Group's

BIBLE SENSE™

EPHESIANS

// SEEING OURSELVES IN JESUS

448-
3683633

Group

Loveland, Colorado
www.group.com

Group resources actually work!

This Group resource helps you focus on **"The 1 Thing®"**—a life-changing relationship with Jesus Christ. "The 1 Thing" incorporates our **R.E.A.L.** approach to ministry. It reinforces a growing friendship with Jesus, encourages long-term learning, and results in life transformation, because it's:

Relational
Learner-to-learner interaction enhances learning and builds Christian friendships.

Experiential
What learners experience through discussion and action sticks with them up to 9 times longer than what they simply hear or read.

Applicable
The aim of Christian education is to equip learners to be both hearers and doers of God's Word.

Learner-based
Learners understand and retain more when the learning process takes into consideration how they learn best.

Group's BIBLESENSE™
EPHESIANS: Seeing Ourselves in Jesus
Copyright © 2006 Group Publishing, Inc.

Visit our Web site: **www.group.com**

Credits
Contributors: Dr. Dave Gallagher, Keith Madsen, A. Koshy Muthalaly, Roxanne Wieman, and Paul Woods
Editor: Carl Simmons
Creative Development Editor: Matt Lockhart
Chief Creative Officer: Joani Schultz
Copy Editor: Linda Marcinkowski
Art Director: Kari K. Monson
Cover Art Director: Jeff A. Storm
Cover Designer: Andrea Filer
Photographer: Rodney Stewart
Production Manager: DeAnne Lear

Unless otherwise indicated, all Scripture quotations are taken from the *Holy Bible,* New Living Translation, copyright © 1996, 2004. Used by permission of Tyndale House Publishers, Inc., Wheaton, Illinois 60189. All rights reserved.

Library of Congress Cataloging-in-Publication Data
Ephesians : seeing ourselves in Jesus.-- 1st American pbk. ed.
      p. cm. -- (Group's BibleSense)
   Includes bibliographical references.
   ISBN-13: 978-0-7644-3241-5 (pbk. : alk. paper)
   1. Bible. N.T. Ephesians--Study and teaching. 2. Bible. N.T. Ephesians--Criticism, interpretation, etc. I. Group Publishing. II. Series.
   BS2695.55.E64 2006
   227'.50071--dc22
                                                2006008357
ISBN: 0-7644-3241-9

10 9 8 7 6 5 4 3 2 1   15 14 13 12 11 10 09 08 07 06
Printed in the United States of America.

CONTENTS

CONTENTS
CONTINUED

INTRODUCTION

TO GROUP'S BIBLESENSE™

Welcome to **Group's BibleSense**™, a book-of-the-Bible series unlike any you've ever seen! This is a Bible study series in which you'll literally be able to *See, Hear, Smell, Taste, and Touch God's Word*—not only through seeing and hearing the actual book of the Bible you're studying on DVD but also through thought-provoking questions and group activities. As you do these sessions, you'll bring the Word to life, bring your group closer together as a community, and help your group members to bring that life to others.

Whether you're new to small groups or have been doing them for years, you'll discover new, exciting, and—dare we say it—*fun* ways to learn and apply God's Word to your life in these sessions. And as you dig deeper into the Bible passage for each session—and its meaning for your life, you'll find your life (and the lives around you) transformed more and more into Jesus' likeness.

Each session concludes with a series of opportunities on how to commit to reaching your world with the Bible passage you've just studied—whether it's in changing your own responses to others, reaching out to them individually or as an entire group, or by taking part in something bigger than your group.

So again, welcome to the world of BibleSense! We hope that you'll find the experiences and studies here both meaningful and memorable, and that as you do them together, your lives will grow even more into the likeness of our Lord, Jesus Christ.

—Carl Simmons, Editor

ABOUT THE SESSIONS

TASTE AND SEE (20 minutes)

Every BibleSense session begins with food—to give group members a chance to unwind and transition from a busy day and other preoccupations into the theme of the session. After the food and a few introductory questions, the group gets to experience Scripture in a fresh way. The passage for each session is included on DVD, as well as in print within the book. Also provided is "A Sense of History," a brief feature offering additional cultural and historical context.

DIGGING INTO SCRIPTURE (30 minutes)

This is the central part of the session. The group will have the chance to interact with the Scripture passage you've just read and watched, and, through questions and other sensory experiences, you'll learn how it applies to *your* life.

MAKING IT PERSONAL (15 minutes)

Now you'll move from understanding how the passage applies to your life, to thinking about ways you *can* apply it. In this part of the session, personal meaning is brought home through meaningful experiences and questions.

TOUCHING YOUR WORLD (25 minutes)

This is the "take home" part of the session. Each group member will choose a weekly challenge to directly apply this session's passage in a practical way in the week ahead, as well as share prayer requests and pray for one another. Also included is a "Taking It Home" section, with tips on how you can prepare for your next session.

GETTING CONNECTED

Pass your books around the room, and have everyone write his or her name, phone number, e-mail address, and birthday.

Name	Phone	E-mail	Birthday
Cindy Buhmer	952-496-1999	mcbuh@earthlink.net	12-08
Liz Volm 13509 Webster Ave	442-1509	volms@integra.net	9/14
Sue	403-9463	suevoegele@hotmail.com	1-7
Julie	496-2215	garten577@msn.com	11/17
Jay Garten	496-2215	Jay.Garten@msn.com	4/17/74
Mary Harbeck	952 994 0954	sharkagirl77@gmail.com	12/17
Jennie Dinsmore	952-496-3995	simplyjennie@comcast.net	8/17
JEFF	612.209-8755	JWDINSMORE@COMCAST.NET	1/2
Kim Voegele	952 403 9463		3/22/1962
Marly R.	496 1999		12/29/53

SESSION 1 :

SEEING YOUR INHERITANCE IN JESUS

In this session you'll discover more about the inheritance we have in Jesus, and how our understanding of that should affect everything we do.

PRE-SESSION CHECKLIST:

☐ **Leader:** Check out the Session 1 Leader Notes in the back of the book (page 95).

☐ **Food Coordinator:** If you are responsible for the Session 1 snack, see page 106.

☐ **Supplies:**

- An uncovered lamp with a bright bulb (60 watt or higher)

TASTE AND SEE (20 minutes)

While enjoying the snack, find a partner—someone you don't know very well—and take a few minutes to tell your partner a couple of things about yourself:

- What was the spiritual environment in the home where you grew up?

> **Write it down!**
>
> *Pass your books around to record each other's contact information (page 7).*

- What kind of spiritual influence have your parents had on you?

Gather back together as a large group. Take turns introducing your partner to the group by sharing one thing you learned about him or her that you didn't already know. Then choose one of the following questions to answer and share with the group:

- What would it be like to have this kind of snack every day?

- Is there such a thing as "too much of a good thing"? Why or why not?

 Watch the first chapter on the DVD (Ephesians 1:1-23). This passage can also be found on the following page if you would like to follow along in your book.

Ephesians 1:1-23

¹This letter is from Paul, chosen by the will of God to be an apostle of Christ Jesus.

I am writing to God's holy people in Ephesus, who are faithful followers of Christ Jesus.

²May God our Father and the Lord Jesus Christ give you grace and peace.

³All praise to God, the Father of our Lord Jesus Christ, who has blessed us with every spiritual blessing in the heavenly realms because we are united with Christ. ⁴Even before he made the world, God loved us and chose us in Christ to be holy and without fault in his eyes. ⁵God decided in advance to adopt us into his own family by bringing us to himself through Jesus Christ. This is what he wanted to do, and it gave him great pleasure. ⁶So we praise God for the glorious grace he has poured out on us who belong to his dear Son. ⁷He is so rich in kindness and grace that he purchased our freedom with the blood of his Son and forgave our sins. ⁸He has showered his kindness on us, along with all wisdom and understanding.

⁹God has now revealed to us his mysterious plan regarding Christ, a plan to fulfill his own good pleasure. ¹⁰And this is the plan: At the right time he will bring everything together under the authority of Christ—everything in heaven and on earth. ¹¹Furthermore, because we are united with Christ, we have received an inheritance from God, for he chose us in advance, and he makes everything work out according to his plan.

¹²God's purpose was that we Jews who were the first to trust in Christ would bring praise and glory to God. ¹³And now you Gentiles have also heard the truth, the Good News that God saves

you. And when you believed in Christ, he identified you as his own by giving you the Holy Spirit, whom he promised long ago. [14]The Spirit is God's guarantee that he will give us the inheritance he promised and that he has purchased us to be his own people. He did this so we would praise and glorify him.

[15]Ever since I first heard of your strong faith in the Lord Jesus and your love for God's people everywhere, [16]I have not stopped thanking God for you. I pray for you constantly, [17]asking God, the glorious Father of our Lord Jesus Christ, to give you spiritual wisdom and insight so that you might grow in your knowledge of God. [18]I pray that your hearts will be flooded with light so that you can understand the confident hope he has given to those he called—his holy people who are his rich and glorious inheritance.

[19]I also pray that you will understand the incredible greatness of God's power for us who believe him. This is the same mighty power [20]that raised Christ from the dead and seated him in the place of honor at God's right hand in the heavenly realms. [21]Now he is far above any ruler or authority or power or leader or anything else—not only in this world but also in the world to come. [22]God has put all things under the authority of Christ and has made him head over all things for the benefit of the church. [23]And the church is his body; it is made full and complete by Christ, who fills all things everywhere with himself.

DIGGING INTO SCRIPTURE (30 minutes)

As a group, discuss:

Tip: *To maximize participation and also to have enough time to work through the session, we recommend breaking into smaller subgroups of three or four at various points during the session.*

• What thoughts or emotions came to your mind while watching this session's Bible passage?

Now break into subgroups.

Subgroup Leaders: Find a place where your subgroup can talk with few distractions. Plan to come back together in 15 minutes.

In your subgroup, read Ephesians 1:1-14 and the following "A Sense of History" feature, and answer the questions that follow.

A SENSE OF HISTORY

Blessings and Challenges at Ephesus

In this letter, written from prison in Rome, the Apostle Paul is writing to a church he may have put more time and energy into than any other church he started. About five years had passed since Paul had left Ephesus, and he was now writing to encourage a church that God was clearly blessing, even in the face of significant opposition. In contrast to the worldly wealth of Ephesus, Paul challenges the church to keep its focus on the many spiritual treasures God bestows to every Christian, "not only in this world but also in the world to come" (verse 21).

Ephesus, a port city in the area that is now Turkey, was one of the largest cities in the Roman Empire. Its temple of the goddess Artemis (Diana)—425 feet long, 200 feet wide, 60 feet high, and supported by 127 columns—was in fact one of the seven wonders of the ancient world. The city even had a tourist industry, with craftsmen creating souvenirs of Artemis for visitors to take home with them. By the time Paul first arrived at Ephesus, the city already depended more on the tourist trade than on harbor traffic, as the harbor had begun filling with silt.

It was in this city, which based much of its prosperity on the false goddess Artemis, that Paul established the Ephesian church. In this letter, he encourages church members to put their trust in their inheritance in Jesus rather than the earthly wealth surrounding them.

- Good food, like this session's snack, can be a blessing to us. What's one blessing in your life that you're *regularly* thankful for?

- In Ephesians 1:3-8, Paul reveals the greatest blessing God's ever given us. What is it? What does that blessing mean to you?

  grace - hope

> "*Mystery creates wonder and wonder is the basis of man's desire to understand.*"
> —*Neil Armstrong*

- Look at verses 9-11. Think of a plan you had that you *thought* was "fail-proof." What happened?

- What's your reaction to Paul's saying that God is willing to share *his* "mysterious," and perfect, plan with *you*?

Come back together as a larger group and share your answers with one another.

Leader: Place the uncovered lamp in the middle of your group.

Darken your room, and then turn on your lamp. Look around and see how the light affects others in your group. Think about how it affects *you*. Then discuss this question:

- If you were lost and alone on a dark night, how would you react to seeing a bright light like this one? Relief? Fear? Something else?

In that light, read Ephesians 1:15-23, and answer the following questions:

- Paul prays that the Ephesians would be "flooded with light" and "understand the incredible greatness of God's power." How is that prayer relevant to you right now?

Did you know?

The candela *is a measurement of light originally called* candlepower *and, as its name suggests, is equal to the power of one candle. A 100-watt bulb gives off approximately 120 candela.*

- What's the connection between understanding who God is and doing what pleases God? How have you seen that in your own life?

MAKING IT PERSONAL (15 minutes)

Re-read Ephesians 1:18-23, and answer these questions:

• How should knowing that you are *God's* inheritance affect the way you approach God?

• How does it (or should it) affect the way you treat *others* who are called God's inheritance? the way you treat those who don't know Jesus?

• What's one practical step you can take right now to "turn up the lights" so you can really see your inheritance in Jesus?

Spend more time

TOUCHING YOUR WORLD (25 minutes)

Review the following "weekly challenge" options, and select the challenge you'd like to do. Turn to a partner, and share your choice. Then make plans to connect with your partner sometime between now and the next session, to check in and encourage one another.

☐ **REFLECT ON YOUR FUTURE.** Spend time reading some passages in your Bible that describe the wonderful future God has planned for you. Start with 2 Thessalonians 1:7, 2 Peter 3:13, and Revelation 21:1-4. Find other passages on your own. Talk with a friend or family member about how the hope of that future should affect the way you live, and commit to working on whatever areas in your life you identify.

☐ **SHARE THE BLESSINGS, PART 1.** Find a practical way to share God's blessings to you with another person. It might be something as small as calling with a word of encouragement or giving a plate of cookies, or as large as making a rent payment for a single mom who's struggling to make ends meet.

☐ **SHARE THE BLESSINGS, PART 2.** Think of a non-Christian you know fairly well who might be ready to hear about your faith. Commit to talking to that person this week, to tell him or her how excited you are about the inheritance and future you have through Jesus.

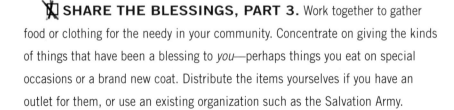 **SHARE THE BLESSINGS, PART 3.** Work together to gather food or clothing for the needy in your community. Concentrate on giving the kinds of things that have been a blessing to *you*—perhaps things you eat on special occasions or a brand new coat. Distribute the items yourselves if you have an outlet for them, or use an existing organization such as the Salvation Army.

Come back together as a group. Share prayer requests. Before the leader prays, take a few moments to silently reflect on God's blessings on your life. *Adoption – Humel the hund – prayers →*

Leader: If you haven't already, take a few minutes to review the group roles and assignments (page 103) with the group. At minimum, be sure that the food and supplies responsibilities for the next session are covered. *Nancy (Liz friend) Brian Hunter Laura*

Libby Rockwell – Mud food distribution (safety) Uncle Art

Until next time...

Date _Sept 30, 2008_

Time _6:30 p.m._

Place _Liz_

Taking It Home:

1. Set a goal for how many times you'll either read through or watch on your DVD the Session 2 Bible passage (Ephesians 2:1-22). Make a point to read the "A Sense of History" feature in Session 2 (page 22) prior to the next session. You may also want to review this week's passage. Let your weekly challenge partner know what goals you've set, so he or she can encourage you and help hold you accountable.

2. Touch base sometime before the next session with your weekly challenge partner to compare notes on how you're both doing with the goals you've set.

3. If you have volunteered for a role or signed up to help with food or supplies for the next session, be sure to prepare for this. The Session 2 Supplies list can be found on page 18, and the Food Coordinator instructions are on page 106.

4. **I commit to touching my world this week by sharing my inheritance in Jesus in the following ways:**

_____

_____

_____

SESSION 2:

BREAKING DOWN WALLS

EPHESIANS 2:1-22

In this session you'll learn how Jesus made it possible for *everyone* to have a relationship with God, and how to knock down the walls that separate *us* from others just as Jesus did.

PRE-SESSION CHECKLIST:

☐ **Leader:** Check out the Session 2 Leader Notes in the back of the book (page 96).

☐ **Food Coordinator:** If you are responsible for the Session 2 snack, see page 106.

☐ **Supplies:**
- Cardboard boxes—enough to build a substantial wall

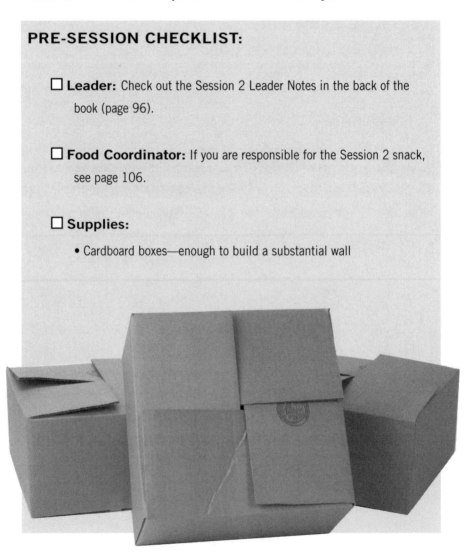

TASTE AND SEE (20 minutes)

You have a couple of different kinds of snacks to choose from today. Choose from one platter or the other—not both—and enjoy your choice. While you're snacking, discuss the following:

• Why did you choose one snack instead of the other?

• Would you have chosen from both platters if you could have? Why or why not?

 Watch the second chapter on the DVD (Ephesians 2:1-22). This passage can also be found on the following page if you would like to follow along in your book.

Ephesians 2:1-22

[1]Once you were dead because of your disobedience and your many sins. [2]You used to live in sin, just like the rest of the world, obeying the devil—the commander of the powers in the unseen world. He is the spirit at work in the hearts of those who refuse to obey God. [3]All of us used to live that way, following the passionate desires and inclinations of our sinful nature. By our very nature we were subject to God's anger, just like everyone else.

[4]But God is so rich in mercy, and he loved us so much, [5]that even though we were dead because of our sins, he gave us life when he raised Christ from the dead. (It is only by God's grace that you have been saved!) [6]For he raised us from the dead along with Christ and seated us with him in the heavenly realms because we are united with Christ Jesus. [7]So God can point to us in all future ages as examples of the incredible wealth of his grace and kindness toward us, as shown in all he has done for us who are united with Christ Jesus.

[8]God saved you by his grace when you believed. And you can't take credit for this; it is a gift from God. [9]Salvation is not a reward for the good things we have done, so none of us can boast about it. [10]For we are God's masterpiece. He has created us anew in Christ Jesus, so we can do the good things he planned for us long ago.

[11]Don't forget that you Gentiles used to be outsiders. You were called "uncircumcised heathens" by the Jews, who were proud of their circumcision, even though it affected only their bodies and not their hearts. [12]In those days you were living apart from Christ. You were excluded from citizenship among the people of Israel, and you did not know the covenant promises God had made to them. You lived in this world without God and without

hope. ¹³But now you have been united with Christ Jesus. Once you were far away from God, but now you have been brought near to him through the blood of Christ.

¹⁴For Christ himself has brought peace to us. He united Jews and Gentiles into one people when, in his own body on the cross, he broke down the wall of hostility that separated us. ¹⁵He did this by ending the system of law with its commandments and regulations. He made peace between Jews and Gentiles by creating in himself one new people from the two groups. ¹⁶Together as one body, Christ reconciled both groups to God by means of his death on the cross, and our hostility toward each other was put to death.

¹⁷He brought this Good News of peace to you Gentiles who were far away from him, and peace to the Jews who were near. ¹⁸Now all of us can come to the Father through the same Holy Spirit because of what Christ has done for us.

¹⁹So now you Gentiles are no longer strangers and foreigners. You are citizens along with all of God's holy people. You are members of God's family. ²⁰Together, we are his house, built on the foundation of the apostles and the prophets. And the cornerstone is Christ Jesus himself. ²¹We are carefully joined together in him, becoming a holy temple for the Lord. ²²Through him you Gentiles are also being made part of this dwelling where God lives by his Spirit.

A SENSE OF HISTORY
A Lasting Feud

Jesus' parting words to the disciples were to "go and make disciples of all the nations" (Matthew 28:19). At first, though, Jesus' disciples limited their message to the Jews. And, in some ways, it was not surprising: The animosity between Jew and Gentile was generations old.

But in Acts 10, God made it very clear to Peter that the Gentiles should no longer be considered unclean (Acts 10:9-16). Peter declared, "I see very clearly that God shows no favoritism. In every nation he accepts those who fear him and do what is right" (Acts 10:34-35). And several verses later (Acts 10:44-48), the Holy Spirit is given to the first of many Gentiles.

But as the number of Gentile converts increased, certain Jewish legalists began to insist that the Gentile Christians must begin following Jewish laws. The Jerusalem Council was assembled to decide what was to be required of the new Gentile Christians. The Council concluded that since the Jews could not be justified by the law, but only by grace, then the Gentile Christians should not be subject to the law either (Acts 15:6-29).

Yet many Jewish Christians continued to resist reaching out to Gentiles—or tried to force the Gentiles to obey Jewish laws and customs. The centuries-old hostility between the Jews and the Gentiles would not easily go away—which was why Paul found it necessary to reassure the Gentiles of their equality in Christ, and to insist that Christ had broken down the wall between Jew and Gentile.

DIGGING INTO SCRIPTURE (30 minutes)

As a group, discuss:

• What thoughts or emotions came to your mind while watching this session's Bible passage, whether just now or during the past week?

Now break into subgroups.

Subgroup Leaders: Find a place where your subgroup can talk with few distractions. Take no more than 15 minutes for your discussion time.

Read Ephesians 2:1-10 together, and answer the following questions:

• Look at verses 1-3. How had the Ephesians been separated from God? What changed, according to verses 4-10?

• In what ways have you experienced the "incredible wealth of [God's] grace and kindness" in your own life?

• What's your reaction to Paul saying that God has specifically created *you* to do good things?

> **Fast fact:** The Berlin Wall, separating East Berlin from West Berlin, is probably the best modern example of a physical wall separating two groups of people. It was knocked down in 1989 after standing as a symbol of the Cold War for 28 years.

Come back together as a larger group and share your answers with one another.

Host: Bring out your cardboard boxes. Recruit some extra hands to help if you need them.

Use the cardboard boxes provided to build a wall. Stand on both sides of your wall so there's room for everyone to work on it. Make it as tall as you can. When you've finished, stay on your side of the wall.

> *"The Jew had an immense contempt for the Gentile. The Gentiles, said the Jews, were created by God to be fuel for the fires of Hell...It was not even lawful to render help to a Gentile mother in her hour of sorest need, for that would simply be to bring another Gentile into the world."*
>
> *—William Barclay*

Read Ephesians 2:11-18, and answer the following questions:

• In what ways does this wall divide you?

• How is this wall like the division that existed between the Jews and Gentiles before Jesus came? How is it different?

Now, as a group, work together to tear down the wall. (Don't break down your boxes, though.) When you've finished, answer the following:

- Look again at Ephesians 2:13-18. How did Jesus break down the wall between Jew and Gentile? How was breaking down your own wall like (or unlike) that?

> *"Mr. Gorbachev, tear down this wall!"*
> —Ronald Reagan, at the Brandenburg Gate, by the Berlin Wall

- What walls do you see in your own community today? How could Jesus use your group to break down those walls? Give some specific examples.

> *"Some of us are Jews, some are Gentiles, some are slaves, and some are free. But we have all been baptized into one body by one Spirit, and we all share the same Spirit."*
> —1 Corinthians 12:13

MAKING IT PERSONAL (15 minutes)

You're going to use your boxes one more time—but instead of a wall, work together as a group to create a *building.* Take no more than five minutes to make your building.

Read Ephesians 2:19-22 and answer the following questions:

• When has God knocked down a wall in your *own* life, then re-used the "bricks" to build something good? Explain.

• What places in your life do you still not feel "carefully joined together" with God's people? with others you come in contact with but tend to avoid?

When you've finished answering, take an extra minute or two to silently reflect and pray about those people God brought to mind during the last question (or as you reflect now). Think of one way God may be asking you to change your approach or response to each person, and resolve to put that into action.

TOUCHING YOUR WORLD (25 minutes)

Review the following weekly challenge options, and select the challenge you'd like to do. Turn to a partner, and share your choice. Then make plans to connect with your partner sometime between now and the next session to check in and encourage one another.

☐ **REFLECT GOD'S MERCY.** Choose this week to consciously reflect God's mercy in your interactions with other people. Read Ephesians 2:1-10 at the beginning of each day, and remember God's mercy to you as you go through the day. Commit to being more forgiving to people who wrong you, more merciful to those who seek mercy, and more conscious of how much we all need mercy.

☐ **GROW GOD'S FAMILY.** Commit to being a faithful part of God's family this week. Find ways to support others in your church or group who are in need—as you would a member of your own family. It might mean taking a pot of soup to someone who's sick, making a phone call to encourage someone who's hurting, or taking a couple of bags of groceries or a gift card to someone who's struggling financially.

☐ **CONNECT WITH AN "OUTSIDER."** Think of someone you know who you don't normally make contact with. Find a way to let him or her know that you care. You might ask a grocery cashier how his or her day is going, or let a coworker know that you're praying about the illness in his or her family. Look for opportunities to share the love of Jesus with them. Commit to begin doing this faithfully, rather than just as a one-time thing.

Cindy-Jay (email)

Come back together as a group. Share prayer requests, and then pray for everyone's needs. Especially pray about ways you can reach "outside the walls" as individuals or as a group this week.

Until next time...

Date _____

Time _____

Place _____

Taking It Home:

1. Set a goal for how many times you'll either read through or watch on your DVD the Session 3 Bible passage (Ephesians 3:1-21). Make a point to read the "A Sense of History" feature in Session 3 (page 33) before the next session. You may also want to review this week's passage—or even watch the entire book of Ephesians straight through. (It takes about 22 minutes.) Let your weekly challenge partner know what goals you've set, so he or she can encourage you and help hold you accountable.

2. Touch base sometime before the next session with your weekly challenge partner to compare notes on how you're both doing with the goals you've set.

3. If you have volunteered for a role or signed up to help with food or supplies for the next session, be sure to prepare for this. The Session 3 Supplies list can be found on page 30, and the Food Coordinator instructions are on page 106.

4. **I commit to touching my world this week by tearing down walls in the following areas:**

_____

_____

_____

_____

_____

_____

SESSION 3:

GETTING IN ON GOD'S SECRET

EPHESIANS 3:1-21

In this session you'll discover how we are all included in God's love, and how to include others in that love as well.

PRE-SESSION CHECKLIST:

☐ **Leader:** Check out the Session 3 Leader Notes in the back of the book (page 97).

☐ **Food Coordinator:** If you are responsible for the Session 3 snack, see page 106.

☐ **Supplies:**

- 1 stick of gum for each person—have two different brands of gum available

- Cup to hold your sticks of gum (deep enough that nothing sticks out)

- 1 penny for each person

- Large bowl of water, filled about halfway

- Towel

TASTE AND SEE (20 minutes)

Today's snack is a very big cookie—but is it big *enough?*

As you're eating, find a partner and share:

• Describe a time in your life when there wasn't enough of something to go around. (It doesn't need to have been a big thing.) What was that like?

Gather back together as a large group, and discuss:

• How was your snack time different from what you were expecting?

• What thoughts crossed your mind while you were being served?

 Watch the third chapter on the DVD (Ephesians 3:1-21). This passage can also be found on the following page.

Ephesians 3:1-21

[1]When I think of all this, I, Paul, a prisoner of Christ Jesus for the benefit of you Gentiles...[2]assuming, by the way, that you know God gave me the special responsibility of extending his grace to you Gentiles. [3]As I briefly wrote earlier, God himself revealed his mysterious plan to me. [4]As you read what I have written, you will understand my insight into this plan regarding Christ. [5]God did not reveal it to previous generations, but now by his Spirit he has revealed it to his holy apostles and prophets.

[6]And this is God's plan: Both Gentiles and Jews who believe the Good News share equally in the riches inherited by God's children. Both are part of the same body, and both enjoy the promise of blessings because they belong to Christ Jesus. [7]By God's grace and mighty power, I have been given the privilege of serving him by spreading this Good News.

[8]Though I am the least deserving of all God's people, he graciously gave me the privilege of telling the Gentiles about the endless treasures available to them in Christ. [9]I was chosen to explain to everyone this mysterious plan that God, the Creator of all things, had kept secret from the beginning.

[10]God's purpose in all this was to use the church to display his wisdom in its rich variety to all the unseen rulers and authorities in the heavenly places. [11]This was his eternal plan, which he carried out through Christ Jesus our Lord.

[12]Because of Christ and our faith in him, we can now come boldly and confidently into God's presence. [13]So please don't lose heart because of my trials here. I am suffering for you, so you should feel honored.

[14]When I think of all this, I fall to my knees and pray to the Father, [15]the Creator of everything in heaven

and on earth. [16]I pray that from his glorious, unlimited resources he will empower you with inner strength through his Spirit. [17]Then Christ will make his home in your hearts as you trust in him. Your roots will grow down into God's love and keep you strong. [18]And may you have the power to understand, as all God's people should, how wide, how long, how high, and how deep his love is. [19]May you experience the love of Christ, though it is too great to understand fully. Then you will be made complete with all the fullness of life and power that comes from God.

[20]Now all glory to God, who is able, through his mighty power at work within us, to accomplish infinitely more than we might ask or think. [21]Glory to him in the church and in Christ Jesus through all generations forever and ever! Amen.

A SENSE OF HISTORY
The Wrong Kind of Mystery

As if opposing "Artemis of the Ephesians" (Acts 19:28) didn't present enough difficulties for Paul, a more subtle opposition came from the Gnostic movements of the time. These sects—many of which wove pieces of Christian belief into their own beliefs—posed a significant problem to the early church during the first few centuries of its history.

Although there were numerous Gnostic sects, which often believed very different things, three teachings were fairly consistent: 1) a belief that matter was evil, and thus Jesus did not actually appear in the flesh; 2) a belief that since the Old Testament God created matter, he too was evil, and thus a separate being from the God of the New Testament; and 3) a belief that the truth—a special knowledge (gnosis)—had been given to them alone, and could be passed along only through "secret" teachings.

Just a few of the early church's responses to these false teachings are found in 2 Peter 2:1, 1 John 4:1-6 and 2 John 5-11. In this passage, Paul answers the Gnostic "truth" with a much larger truth: God has chosen to make the mystery of his love available to everyone who puts trust in Jesus.

DIGGING INTO SCRIPTURE (30 minutes)

As a group, discuss:

- What thoughts or emotions came to your mind while watching this session's Bible passage, whether just now or during the past week?

 Leader: Take the cup you prepared, and let group members each draw a stick of gum. Don't let anyone peek!

The person who drew the *different* stick of gum is the odd one out.

Leader: Show your "outsider" where he or she has been "exiled" to, and return to the group, leaving him or her behind.

As a group, discuss a "hot topic"—something in the news, or a special occasion in someone's life. But don't include your "outsider" in the conversation.

After a minute or two of discussion, get out of your seats. As a group, rally around your outcast group member and bring him or her back into the group.

Discuss the following:

- **To the person who was excluded:** What was it like to be left out of the discussion?

- **To everyone else:** What were you thinking as you kept that person out of the discussion?

Now break into subgroups.

Subgroup Leaders: Find a place where your subgroup can talk with few distractions. Take no more than 15 minutes for your discussion time.

Read Ephesians 3:1-13, and answer the following questions:

• How do you think the Gentiles in Ephesus reacted the first time they read this part of their letter from Paul?

Suspicious

• Whom do you see as the spiritually disconnected in our society? in your community?

• What things tend to keep us from following Paul's lead and reaching out to others (especially to those of a different race or culture), and telling them "about the endless treasures available to them in Christ"?

forcing beliefs on others?

> **"The churches we surveyed were often myopic, at first. Then they began looking outside their walls. Soon they saw spiritually disconnected people everywhere."**
> — "Back from the Brink," Leadership magazine

Come back together as a larger group and share any highlights or questions from your subgroup discussion.

MAKING IT PERSONAL (15 minutes)

Stay together as a larger group.

Host: Set out the bowl with water in it, and give everyone a penny. Put the bowl on a towel, so water doesn't splash onto your furniture or floor.

Close your eyes, make a wish, and toss your penny into the bowl of water. (For an extra challenge, see how far away you can stand and still get the penny in the bowl!)

Read Ephesians 3:14-21, and answer these questions:

• What's the difference between making a wish by tossing a penny, and offering your prayers to God?

• Paul says in verse 20 that God is "able, through his mighty power at work within us, to accomplish infinitely more than we might ask or think." Do you really believe that? Why or why not?

• When have you experienced, or caught a glimpse into, "how wide, how long, how high, and how deep [God's] love is"? What can we do to better understand—and remember—the width, length, height, and depth of God's love?

TOUCHING YOUR WORLD (25 minutes)

Review the following weekly challenge options, and select the challenge you'd like to do. Turn to a partner, and share your choice. Then make plans to connect with your partner sometime between now and the next session to check in and encourage one another.

☐ **GIVE GOD YOUR TIME.** Set aside a time each day to talk to God. Ask God for the things that are on your heart, and ask God to help you know the things that are on *his* heart. Remember, God wants "to accomplish infinitely more than we might ask or think." Don't limit your prayers to what you *think* you need—ask God to show you what he *can* (and what he *wants to*) do in your life. The answers will probably surprise you.

☐ **INCLUDE EVERYONE.** Jesus did it—and so should you. Think of someone in your life who is a challenge to love—someone you regularly (intentionally or not) exclude from your life. Do something to include that person. Invite him or her to lunch with you and a group of friends. Ask about his or her week, and *really listen* to the answer. Whatever you do, pray first, and ask God to help you remember that his love includes everyone.

☐ **SHARE THE GOOD NEWS.** It's the most important news you could ever share! This week, treat it that way. Be hopeful because God has given you eternal life—and when others ask about your hope and your excitement, tell them what God has done for you! Intentionally look for natural opportunities to share.

Come back together as a group. Share prayer requests. Have your Prayer Coordinator open your prayer time by re-reading Ephesians 3:14-21, and then pray for everyone's needs. Make sure that everyone in your group is prayed for, whether they have a specific prayer request or not.

Until next time...

Date _Oct 21 (Tuesday)_

Time _6:30_

Place _1276 Monroe_

Taking It Home:

1. Set a goal for how many times you'll either read through or watch on your DVD the Session 4 Bible passage (Ephesians 4:1-16). Make a point of reading the "A Sense of History" feature in Session 4 (page 43) before the next session. You may also want to review this week's passage—or even watch the entire book of Ephesians straight through. (It takes about 22 minutes.) Let your weekly challenge partner know what goals you've set, so he or she can encourage you and help hold you accountable.

2. Touch base sometime before the next session with your weekly challenge partner to compare notes on how you're both doing with the goals you've set.

3. If you have volunteered for a role or signed up to help with food or supplies for the next session, be sure to prepare for this. The Session 4 Supplies list can be found on page 40, and the Food Coordinator instructions are on page 107.

4. **I commit to touching my world this week by including others in the secret of God's love in the following ways:**

_____

_____

_____

_____

_____

_____

*Jackie – 16 – Hastings Hospital → Kidney Stones
(hospital)

*Cheyenne → Bishop
* Kate (Uay M to Staples) – 16 –
* G. Cassie Ganderson – Motorcycle – 19 yrs old
  accident
  – Safety → roofing*

SESSION 4:

PREPARING THE BODY

EPHESIANS 4:1-16

In this session you'll explore how Jesus has brought all Christians together as a body, and how *you* can help prepare and strengthen that body.

PRE-SESSION CHECKLIST:

☐ **Leader:** Check out the Session 4 Leader Notes in the back of the book (page 98).

☐ **Food Coordinator:** If you are responsible for the Session 4 snack, see page 107.

☐ **Supplies:**

- Belts—one for each person

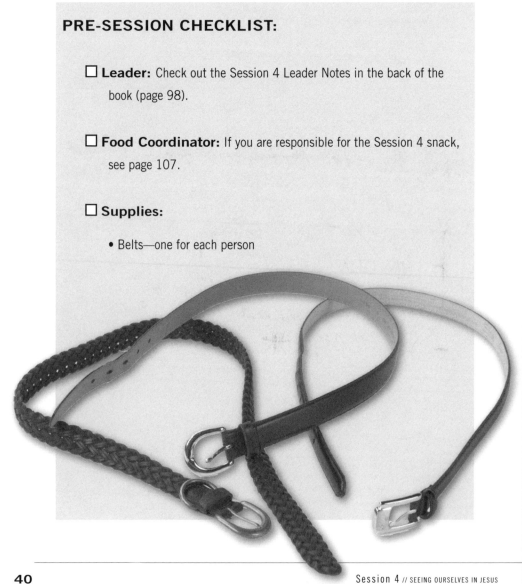

TASTE AND SEE (20 minutes)

While you're enjoying some food, turn to a partner and share:

• When did your first impressions of someone turn out to be totally wrong (in a positive way)? What initially "turned you off"?

• What happened to change your perspective about that person?

Gather back together as a large group, and answer the following:

• Which platter of food did you find yourself choosing from more than the other? Why?

 Watch the fourth chapter on the DVD (Ephesians 4:1-16).

Ephesians 4:1-16

[1]Therefore I, a prisoner for serving the Lord, beg you to lead a life worthy of your calling, for you have been called by God. [2]Always be humble and gentle. Be patient with each other, making allowance for each other's faults because of your love. [3]Make every effort to keep yourselves united in the Spirit, binding yourselves together with peace. [4]For there is one body and one Spirit, just as you have been called to one glorious hope for the future. [5]There is one Lord, one faith, one baptism, [6]and one God and Father, who is over all and in all and living through all.

[7]However, he has given each one of us a special gift through the generosity of Christ. [8]That is why the Scriptures say,

"When he ascended to the heights,
he led a crowd of captives
and gave gifts to his people."

[9]Notice that it says "he ascended." This clearly means that Christ also descended to our lowly world. [10]And the same one who descended is the one who ascended higher than all the heavens, so that he might fill the entire universe with himself.

[11]Now these are the gifts Christ gave to the church: the apostles, the prophets, the evangelists, and the pastors and teachers. [12]Their responsibility is to equip God's people to do his work and build up the church, the body of Christ. [13]This will continue until we all come to such unity in our

faith and knowledge of God's Son that we will be mature in the Lord, measuring up to the full and complete standard of Christ.

[14]Then we will no longer be immature like children. We won't be tossed and blown about by every wind of new teaching. We will not be influenced when people try to trick us with lies so clever they sound like the truth. [15]Instead, we will speak the truth in love, growing in every way more and more like Christ, who is the head of his body, the church. [16]He makes the whole body fit together perfectly. As each part does its own special work, it helps the other parts grow, so that the whole body is healthy and growing and full of love.

A SENSE OF HISTORY

Reconciling Differences

In a time where we often speak of "multicultural ministry," there are few examples better than the one Paul left through his accomplishments in the book of Acts, and in his letters to the churches he helped start. Paul's missionary journeys took the good news of Jesus from Jerusalem to Arabia (Galatians 1:17), throughout Asia Minor, Macedonia, Greece, Italy, Mediterranean islands such as Crete and Malta, and possibly even as far as Spain (Romans 15:28). He had once boasted, "I have become all things to all men so that by all possible means I might save some" (1 Corinthians 9:22, New International Version), and he had the résumé to back it up.

Paul's desire to bring different people together in Christ is even reflected in his name. Because he was the son of a Jew who was also a Roman citizen, and he grew up in the Greek-speaking city of Tarsus, some scholars believe he had both names—Saul and Paul—from birth. Small wonder, then, that God would also use Paul to bring different peoples together through his ministry.

DIGGING INTO SCRIPTURE (30 minutes)

As a group, discuss:

• What thoughts or emotions came to your mind while watching this session's Bible passage?

Now break into subgroups.

Check it out!

Contrary to what many assume, Saul's name didn't change to Paul on the road to Damascus. Read the story again, on your own time, in Acts 9. In fact, Saul doesn't start being called Paul until Acts 13—many years after his Damascus experience.

Subgroup Leaders: Take no more than 15 minutes for your discussion time.

Read Ephesians 4:1-6, and answer the following questions:

• According to this passage, in what ways is there *already* unity in the church?

• Describe a time you tried to go it alone—without being connected with a church or group—whether before or since you knew Jesus. What was it like?

• Now describe a time when you've experienced God bringing a church or group together for a purpose. What was *that* like? What was the difference between those two experiences?

Come back together as a larger group, and share any highlights or questions from your subgroup discussion.

Verse 3 says to "make every effort to keep yourselves united in the Spirit, binding yourselves together." It's time to take the latter part of this command literally. Remove your belts (those of you who are wearing them), and work together as a group to fasten all your belts together so they make *one big* belt.

Did you know? *The average human body has 206 bones and 656 muscles. Each has its own important function. If you don't believe it, try not using some of those parts.*

Host: Bring out your other belts at this time, if your group needs them.

Wrap your big belt around your entire group—work together so everyone is relatively comfortable. While you're bound together, take a mental picture of the moment. Then let your group loose, sit back down, and answer the following questions:

• What were you thinking when you took your "picture" of the group with this big, odd belt around it?

"*All the blessings we enjoy are Divine deposits, committed to our trust on this condition, that they should be dispensed for the benefit of our neighbors.***"**
—*John Calvin*, The Institutes of the Christian Religion

• How is this belt like the unity you read about in verses 1-6? How *isn't* it?

> "*Connection happens when we place the right people in the right places for the right reasons at the right time.*"
> —*Sue Mallory*, The Equipping Church

• The belt you wore kept you restricted. How does spiritual unity actually *free* you, in real life?

• How should knowing that all Christians are part of one body affect the way we approach other Christians?

MAKING IT PERSONAL (15 minutes)

Read Ephesians 4:7-16, and answer these questions:

• In your time together as a group so far, what gifts or talents have you recognized in each other? Be specific.

• What's one gift, talent, or ability you have that you intentionally try to use to serve the body of Christ? to serve those who *don't* yet know Jesus?

Did you know?

*God gives "spiritual gifts" to **all** his children. Read Romans 12:6-8, 1 Corinthians 12, and I Peter 4:10-11 on your own time, and find a leader in your group or church who can help you discover how God has gifted you.*

• What other natural abilities or strengths do you have? How do you think *those* could be used to serve God and others?

TOUCHING YOUR WORLD (25 minutes)

Review the following weekly challenge options, and select the challenge you'd like to do. Turn to a partner, and share your choice. Then make plans to connect with your partner sometime between now and the next session to check in and encourage one another.

☐ **SPEAK THE TRUTH IN LOVE.** Look for an opportunity where you can speak the truth in love to someone (Ephesians 4:15) this week. Be prayerful and sensitive as you do this. You may need to speak the truth in love by being assertive (not aggressive or defensive) with someone who needs to hear truthful, caring words that may be difficult for you to share (and for that person to hear). On the other hand, the truth doesn't always hurt. This may be a good opportunity to use the truth to encourage your spouse or children, or to send a thank-you card to a friend to affirm the gifts that he or she brings to your friendship.

☐ **USE YOUR SPIRITUAL GIFT FOR GOD'S GLORY THIS WEEK.** If you know your spiritual gift, identify a way to use that gift in the coming week. If you're not sure what your spiritual gift is, set up a time to talk with your pastor, staff member, or group leader (if he or she is equipped to do it). Ask him or her to help you discover what your gift is and how you can use it.

☐ **GET OUT OF YOUR COMFORT ZONE.** Take this next week to think about how you could stretch your boundaries. Is there a leadership role you could help fill? Is there some service project you could get involved in? Is there a ministry in your church where you could give someone a much-needed break this week? Commit to taking that step and to contacting those people who could help you further serve the body of Christ.

Come back together as a group. Share prayer requests, and then pray for everyone's needs. Take some extra time tonight to thank God for each person in the group and the special contribution they bring to it just by showing up.

—Noah/wife

Until next time...

Date _____

Time _____

Place _____

Taking It Home:

1. Set a goal for how many times you'll either read through or watch on your DVD the Session 5 Bible passage (Ephesians 4:17-32). Make a point to read the "A Sense of History" feature in Session 5 (page 53) before the next session. You may also want to review this week's passage—or even watch the entire book of Ephesians straight through. (It takes about 22 minutes.) Let your weekly challenge partner know what goals you've set, so he or she can encourage you and help hold you accountable.

2. Touch base sometime before the next session with your weekly challenge partner to compare notes on how you're both doing with the goals you've set.

3. If you have volunteered for a role or signed up to help with food or supplies for the next session, be sure to prepare for this. The Session 5 Supplies list can be found on page 50, and the Food Coordinator instructions are on page 107.

4. **I commit to touching my world this week by serving the body of Christ in the following ways:**

_____

_____

_____

_____

SESSION 5:

BECOMING A NEW PERSON IN JESUS

EPHESIANS 4:17-32

In this session you'll learn more about what it means to live as a new person in Jesus.

PRE-SESSION CHECKLIST:

☐ **Leader:** Check out the Session 5 Leader Notes in the back of the book (page 99).

☐ **Food Coordinator:** If you are responsible for the Session 5 snack, see page 107.

☐ **Supplies:**
- 1 old, beat-up jacket
- 1 new jacket

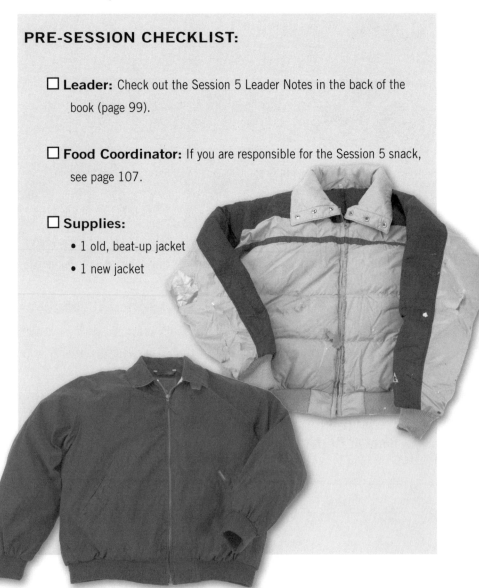

TASTE AND SEE (20 minutes)

While enjoying the snack, find a partner and discuss the following:

• What's one thing that (in general) really makes you mad?

Gather back together as a large group, and share what you discovered about each other. Then discuss the following questions:

• Which dough did you choose—fully baked, partially baked, or unbaked? Why?

• How would you describe your own spiritual state right now? Unbaked? Partially baked? Baked to a golden brown? Burnt to a crisp? Explain your answer.

 Watch the fifth chapter on the DVD (Ephesians 4:17-32).

Ephesians 4:17-32

[17]With the Lord's authority I say this: Live no longer as the Gentiles do, for they are hopelessly confused. [18]Their minds are full of darkness; they wander far from the life God gives because they have closed their minds and hardened their hearts against him. [19]They have no sense of shame. They live for lustful pleasure and eagerly practice every kind of impurity.

[20]But that isn't what you learned about Christ. [21]Since you have heard about Jesus and have learned the truth that comes from him, [22]throw off your old sinful nature and your former way of life, which is corrupted by lust and deception. [23]Instead, let the Spirit renew your thoughts and attitudes. [24]Put on your new nature, created to be like God—truly righteous and holy.

[25]So stop telling lies. Let us tell our neighbors the truth, for we are all parts of the same body. [26]And "don't sin by letting anger control you." Don't let the sun go down while you are still angry, [27]for anger gives a foothold to the devil.

[28]If you are a thief, quit stealing. Instead, use your hands for good hard work, and then give generously to others in need.
[29]Don't use foul or abusive language. Let everything you say be good and helpful, so that your words will be an encouragement to those who hear them.

[30]And do not bring sorrow to God's Holy Spirit by the way you live. Remember, he has identified you as his own, guaranteeing that you will be saved on the day of redemption.

[31]Get rid of all bitterness, rage, anger, harsh words, and slander, as well as all types of evil behavior. [32]Instead, be kind to each other, tenderhearted, forgiving one another, just as God through Christ has forgiven you.

A SENSE OF HISTORY

The Price of New Life

Paul spent more than two years in Ephesus, telling others of the new life in Jesus Christ. By preaching that "handmade gods aren't really gods at all" (Acts 19:26), he was slowly putting silversmiths who created images of Artemis out of business—and those silversmiths weren't happy.

Acts 19 tells us of a man named Demetrius, who gathered his fellow craftsmen together and told them Paul was ruining their livelihood. Demetrius stirred up the silversmiths, who in turn stirred up the rest of the city, and riots soon broke out. Other Christians prevented Paul from confronting the rioters, but two other missionaries, Gaius and Aristarchus, were dragged into the amphitheater. Fortunately the mayor of Ephesus persuaded the rioters that the Roman government might not be pleased by their rioting, and the crowd soon dispersed. (Read the whole story, on your own time—it's a fascinating portrait of just one of the many challenges the early church faced.)

Timothy, Paul's protégé, later became the first bishop of the Ephesian church. Tradition teaches that Timothy later paid the ultimate price for opposing Artemis-worship, being martyred about A.D. 97.

DIGGING INTO SCRIPTURE (30 minutes)

As a group, discuss:

• What thoughts or emotions came to your mind while watching this session's Bible passage?

Now break into subgroups.

Subgroup Leaders: Agree to come back together in 10 minutes.

Read Ephesians 4:17-24, and answer the following questions:

• In what ways do you already think of yourself as a new person in Jesus? What helps you to see your "newness" in those areas of your life?

• In what ways is it hard to see yourself as a new person in Jesus?

Come back together as a larger group and share any highlights or questions from your subgroup discussion.

Leader: Bring out your old and new jackets.

Everyone should try on the old jacket first. Take a whiff of it, even; get a feel for where this jacket has been.

Now have everyone try on the new jacket.

> "This means that anyone who belongs to Christ has become a new person. The old life is gone; a new life has begun!"
> —2 Corinthians 5:17

Once everyone's tried both jackets on, answer the following questions:

• How comfortable were you when trying each jacket on? Which one felt better? Why?

• How was trying on and taking off each jacket like the changing of the "old life" for the "new life" that Paul describes in verses 22-24? How is it different?

• How easy or difficult has it been for you to "throw off... your former way of life," and "let the Spirit renew your thoughts and attitudes"? Explain.

• Who's an example of someone you know whose life was radically changed by Jesus? What about this person would you like to better emulate in your own life?

MAKING IT PERSONAL (15 minutes)

Read Ephesians 4:25-32, and answer the following questions:

• How can your communication with others change so it becomes more "good and helpful"—so it builds others up rather than tears them down?

• Where is anger "controlling" your relationship with someone you know right now? What's one thing you can do to change that?

> **Check it out!** *Paul's letter isn't the last mention of the church at Ephesus in the Bible. On your own time, read Revelation 2:1-7, and discover how God used the Apostle John to give a powerful wake-up call to the Ephesian church.*

• Are there any other areas of your life where you sense you may be "bring[ing] sorrow to God's Holy Spirit"? If so, what changes do you need to make to bring your new life in Jesus into those areas?

TOUCHING YOUR WORLD (25 minutes)

Review the following weekly challenge options, and select the challenge you'd like to do. Turn to a partner, and share your choice. Then make plans to connect with your partner sometime between now and the next session to check in and encourage one another.

☐ **KEEP A JOURNAL FOR ONE WEEK.** For the next seven days, jot down experiences where you've needed to make a stand for Jesus—such as sharing your faith story, or keeping your integrity in a difficult situation. Write how God helped you gain victory—maybe a Christian friend encouraged you, or God brought a Scripture verse to mind to give you strength. (And if you had problems keeping your stand, be honest and write *that* down, and ask God for help.)

☐ **GET VICTORY OVER ANGER.** Write Ephesians 4:26-27 down on a small piece of paper. Read it at the beginning of each day, and carry it with you this next week. Be prepared for that moment of anger that will probably come your way. As soon as it creeps into your mind, take out your slip of paper and re-read it. Pray for God's strength, and claim God's promise of victory. If you *did* express anger unjustly, go to the person involved and ask his or her forgiveness.

☐ **ENCOURAGE ONE PERSON THIS WEEK.** Watch for opportunities God gives you to encourage someone with your words this week. When you see the opportunity, go to that person and share something very specific that will be a real encouragement to him or her. If you're married, watch for an opportunity to encourage your spouse. If you have children, watch for an opportunity to encourage your child. Be alert to opportunities to come alongside co-workers or neighbors who need encouragement as well. Share Jesus' love, so others can know it, too.

Come back together as a group. Share prayer requests, and if you're comfortable doing so, share which weekly challenge you selected this week, as well as other ways you sense you need to experience the new life that Jesus offers us. Then pray for everyone's needs.

Until next time...

Date _____

Time _____

Place _____

Taking It Home:

1. Set a goal for how many times you'll either read through or watch on your DVD the Session 6 Bible passage (Ephesians 5:1-20). Make a point to read the "A Sense of History" feature in Session 6 (page 63) before the next session. You may also want to review this week's passage—or even watch the entire book of Ephesians straight through. (It takes about 22 minutes.) Let your weekly challenge partner know what goals you've set, so he or she can encourage you and help hold you accountable.

2. Touch base sometime before the next session with your weekly challenge partner to compare notes on how you're both doing with the goals you've set.

3. If you have volunteered for a role or signed up to help with food or supplies for the next session, be sure to prepare for this. The Session 6 Supplies list can be found on page 60, and the Food Coordinator instructions are on page 107.

4. **I commit to touching my world this week by bringing the new life of Jesus into *my* life in the following ways:**

_____

_____

_____

_____

SESSION 6:

FOLLOWING JESUS' EXAMPLE

EPHESIANS 5:1-20

In this session you'll focus on how to make choices for Jesus, and how to continue to make them each day.

PRE-SESSION CHECKLIST:

☐ **Leader:** Check out the Session 6 Leader Notes in the back of the book (page 100).

☐ **Food Coordinator:** If you are responsible for the Session 6 snack, see page 107.

☐ **Supplies:**
- None

TASTE AND SEE (20 minutes)

Your snack for this session is trail mix. Maybe you'll like everything in the mix; maybe you won't. Take what you like and leave what you don't.

As you're eating, find a partner and share:

• What was one choice you had to make—or at least had to work on making—today?

Gather back together as a large group, and choose one of the following questions to answer and share with the group:

• Which parts of the trail mix did you like best? Which parts, if any, did you leave behind? Why?

• How was choosing what parts of your snack to enjoy similar to other choices you make each day?

 Watch the sixth chapter on the DVD (Ephesians 5:1-20).

Ephesians 5:1-20

[1]Imitate God, therefore, in everything you do, because you are his dear children. [2]Live a life filled with love, following the example of Christ. He loved us and offered himself as a sacrifice for us, a pleasing aroma to God.

[3]Let there be no sexual immorality, impurity, or greed among you. Such sins have no place among God's people. [4]Obscene stories, foolish talk, and coarse jokes—these are not for you. Instead, let there be thankfulness to God. [5]You can be sure that no immoral, impure, or greedy person will inherit the Kingdom of Christ and of God. For a greedy person is an idolater, worshiping the things of this world.

[6]Don't be fooled by those who try to excuse these sins, for the anger of God will fall on all who disobey him. [7]Don't participate in the things these people do. [8]For once you were full of darkness, but now you have light from the Lord. So live as people of light! [9]For this light within you produces only what is good and right and true.

[10]Carefully determine what pleases the Lord. [11]Take no part in the worthless deeds of evil and darkness; instead, expose them. [12]It is shameful even to talk about the things that ungodly people do in secret. [13]But their evil intentions will be exposed when the light shines on them, [14]for the light makes everything visible. This is why it is said,

"Awake, O sleeper,
rise up from the dead,
and Christ will give you light."
[15]So be careful how you live.

Don't live like fools, but like those who are wise. [16]Make the most of every opportunity in these evil days. [17]Don't act thoughtlessly, but understand what the Lord wants you to do. [18]Don't be drunk with wine, because that will ruin your life. Instead, be filled with the Holy Spirit, [19]singing psalms and hymns and spiritual songs among yourselves, and making music to the Lord in your hearts. [20]And give thanks for everything to God the Father in the name of our Lord Jesus Christ.

A SENSE OF HISTORY

The Theater at Ephesus

The amphitheater, or public stadium, was often the largest outdoor building in any Roman city, and the theater of Ephesus was no exception. The amphitheater, which was the site of the riots described in Acts 19, contained about 25,000 seats and was believed to hold as many as 50,000 spectators.

Construction on the amphitheater began around the first half of the third century B.C., and was added onto regularly until the great earthquake of A.D. 262 collapsed parts of it. Remains of the amphitheater can still be seen today.

Worship of pagan gods in such public arenas was very profitable because it brought in large numbers of people from the major cities. The theater also featured gladiatorial fights between men and wild beasts. Although no direct connection with the theater in Ephesus has been established, it was also in open theaters like this elsewhere in the Roman Empire that many of the earliest martyrs of the Christian faith lost their lives.

DIGGING INTO SCRIPTURE (30 minutes)

As a group, discuss:

• What thoughts or emotions came to your mind while watching this session's Bible passage?

Now break into subgroups.

Subgroup Leaders: Plan to come back together in 15 minutes.

Read Ephesians 5:1-9, and answer the following questions:

• Who was your hero, or a person you modeled yourself after, when you were younger? Why did you choose that person?

• According to this passage, in what ways are we to imitate God? In what ways has God enabled us to do that?

• Describe a time you had to make a difficult choice and knew what the right decision was. What helped you to finally make your choice? What thoughts and emotions did you experience both before and after making your choice?

Come back together as a larger group and share any highlights or questions from your subgroup discussion.

 Play a quick round of Simon Says! Take turns leading.

Then sit back down and answer the following questions:

• How easy or difficult was it to imitate the things your leader(s) did?

• How easy or difficult is it for you to follow someone else's example in real life? Why?

• In what ways is it difficult for you to follow Jesus' example? Who or what could help you in following Jesus' example?

MAKING IT PERSONAL (15 minutes)

Play one more round of Simon Says, with just one leader this time. Keep the round short (two minutes at the most). But this time, whatever the leader asks for, *everyone else should do the opposite thing.*

When you've finished, answer the following questions:

• What did you enjoy about doing the opposite of what your leader did? What was not so enjoyable?

• How were your concepts of *opposite* similar? different? What surprised you about this?

Read Ephesians 5:10-20, and answer the following questions:

• When should you listen to what others have to say, but *not* follow their example? What are the consequences of not conforming to what others want?

• Where do you struggle in discerning between what are "worthless deeds of evil and darkness" and "what pleases the Lord"? What is one thing you can do—or who is one person you can confide in—to help you work through these struggles?

TOUCHING YOUR WORLD (25 minutes)

Review the following weekly challenge options, and select the challenge you'd like to do. Turn to a partner, and share your choice. Then make plans to connect with your partner sometime between now and the next session to check in and encourage one another.

☐ **ADDRESS YOUR WEAK SPOTS.** Recognize that you may face difficult choices every day. Commit to seeking Jesus' help in making those choices. Commit to praying specifically for those choices each day, and enlist the help of a friend to join you in prayer and encouragement in those areas—maybe the person you're paired with right now.

☐ **GET AN ACCOUNTABILITY PARTNER.** Make a long-term commitment to get together regularly with someone else who's trying to become more like Jesus. Commit to meeting on a regular basis with that person (for a few months, at the minimum), so you can strengthen and challenge one another through prayer, friendship, and support. You might even be partnered with that person right now.

☐ **STRENGTHEN A FRIEND.** Is there a friend or co-worker who's facing a difficult choice? Commit to praying for that person specifically about the choices he or she has to make, and let him or her know you're praying for them. If it's appropriate, put that person in touch with members of your group or church who might be able to help. It would come as a pleasant surprise.

Come back together as a group. Share prayer requests, and then pray for everyone's needs. If there are group members facing especially hard choices right now, make sure you take the opportunity to pray for each of them and to follow up with them during the week.

Until next time...

Date _____

Time _____

Place _____

Taking It Home:

1. Set a goal for how many times you'll either read through or watch on your DVD the Session 7 Bible passage (Ephesians 5:21–6:9). Make a point to read the "A Sense of History" feature in Session 7 (page 74) before the next session. You may also want to review this week's passage—or even watch the entire book of Ephesians straight through. (It takes about 22 minutes.) Let your weekly challenge partner know what goals you've set, so he or she can encourage you and help hold you accountable.

2. Touch base sometime before the next session with your weekly challenge partner to compare notes on how you're both doing with the goals you've set.

3. If you have volunteered for a role or signed up to help with food or supplies for the next session, be sure to prepare for this. The Session 7 Supplies list can be found on page 70, and the Food Coordinator instructions are on page 107.

4. **I commit to touching my world this week by making the following choices in my walk with Jesus:**

_____

_____

_____

_____

_____

_____

SESSION 7: LOVING, CARING, AND HONORING EACH OTHER

EPHESIANS 5:21–6:9

In this session you'll explore what submission *really* looks like in God's kingdom, and some practical ways you can live it out.

PRE-SESSION CHECKLIST:

☐ **Leader:** Check out the Session 7 Leader Notes in the back of the book (page 101).

☐ **Food Coordinator:** If you are responsible for the Session 7 snack, see page 107.

☐ **Supplies:**

- Cups and glasses for everyone in the group (for an activity—not for the snack)

- Paper plates for everyone

- Variety of items that could have symbolic meaning for group members (include such things as rocks, leaves, CDs or DVDs, spice jars, alarm clocks, cell phones, stuffed animals, or candles)

- 1 stick of modeling clay or small can of Play-Doh for each person

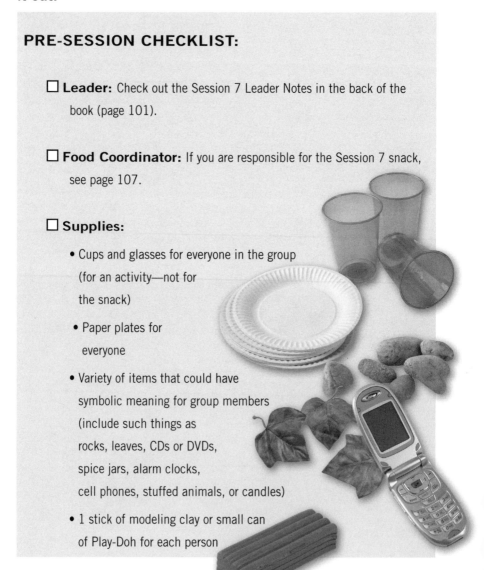

TASTE AND SEE (20 minutes)

This session's snack is a choice of four different flavors of ice cream. However, *your neighbor*—not you—will choose your snack. Choose for the person on your right, and serve your choice to him or her—with no discussion of preferences.

Eat the ice cream that your neighbor has chosen for you. As you eat, discuss the following:

- Why did you choose that specific kind of ice cream for your neighbor?

- How did you like what your neighbor chose for you? What would *you* have chosen?

- What made you less comfortable—choosing ice cream for someone else, or having someone else choose for you? Why?

 Watch the seventh chapter on the DVD (Ephesians 5:21–6:9).

Ephesians 5:21–6:9

Everyone

21And further, submit to one another out of reverence for Christ.

Women

22For wives, this means submit to your husbands as to the Lord. 23For a husband is the head of his wife as Christ is the head of the church. He is the Savior of his body, the church. 24As the church submits to Christ, so you wives should submit to your husbands in everything.

Guys

25For husbands, this means love your wives, just as Christ loved the church. He gave up his life for her 26to make her holy and clean, washed by the cleansing of God's word. 27He did this to present her to himself as a glorious church without a spot or wrinkle or any other blemish. Instead, she will be holy and without fault. 28In the same way, husbands ought to love their wives as they love their own bodies. For a man who loves his wife actually shows love for himself. 29No one hates his own body but feeds and cares for it, just as Christ cares for the church. 30And we are members of his body.

31As the Scriptures say, "A man leaves his father and mother and is joined to his wife, and the two are united into one." 32This is a great mystery, but it is an illustration of the way Christ and the church are one. 33So again I say, each man must love his wife as he loves himself, and the wife must respect her husband.

6:1Children, obey your parents because you belong to the Lord, for this is the right thing to do. 2"Honor your father and mother." This is the first commandment with a promise: 3If you honor your father and mother, "things will go well for you, and you will have a long life on the earth."

parents

4Fathers, do not provoke your children to anger by the way you treat them. Rather, bring them up with the discipline and instruction that comes from the Lord.

5Slaves, obey your earthly masters with deep respect and fear. Serve them sincerely as you would serve Christ. 6Try to please them all the time, not just when they are watching you. As slaves of Christ, do the will of God with all your heart. 7Work with enthusiasm, as though you were working for the Lord rather than for people. 8Remember that the Lord will reward each one of us for the good we do, whether we are slaves or free.

*All
Everyone
employed
by someone
else*

9Masters, treat your slaves in the same way. Don't threaten them; remember, you both have the same Master in heaven, and he has no favorites.

A SENSE OF HISTORY
Changing Domestic Life

How does domestic life in Paul's time compare to today? There were certainly cultural differences: Women in Roman and Greek society could divorce their husbands, while women in Jewish society generally could not; and women in Roman and Greek societies generally had more freedom in owning property and doing business. The Philippian woman Lydia, who had her own business selling dyed cloth (Acts 16:14-15), probably wouldn't have had that opportunity in Jerusalem. Nonetheless, women in all cultures were generally treated as second-class citizens.

Love was less central to marriage at this time, particularly in Roman society. Marriage was a practical necessity for providing a man offspring. As one historian writes concerning Roman society, "Love in marriage was a stoke of good fortune, it was not the basis of the institution." (as quoted in *A History of Private Life: From Pagan Rome to Byzantium*, edited by Paul Veyne)

Children were also treated largely as possessions. In Roman and Greek society, the father could have a newborn baby thrown out on the city garbage dump if he didn't want the child. Those children who didn't die were picked up by slave traders and raised as slaves. While such acts were not allowed in Jewish society, children still had no rights of their own— which was why Jesus' insistence on allowing little children to come to him was so significant (Matthew 19:13-15).

In such a time—and sometimes just as much today—Paul's call for husbands to love their wives in a self-sacrificial way, and to treat their children gently, was a call to revolutionary change.

DIGGING INTO SCRIPTURE (30 minutes)

As a group, discuss:

• What thoughts or emotions came to your mind while watching this session's Bible passage?

Read Ephesians 5:21–6:9 as a choral reading, as follows:

Everyone: Read 5:21 together.

Women only: Read 5:22-24.

Men only: Read 5:25-33.

Parents only: Read 6:1-4.

Everyone who is employed by someone else: Read 6:5-9.

Do this without any breaks between sections.

Now break into subgroups.

Subgroup Leaders: Take 15 minutes for your discussion time.

Answer the following questions:

• Some form of the word *submit* is used four times in the first four verses of this passage. What's your reaction to that word? What personal experiences, positive or negative, does it bring to mind?

• What's the connection between *submitting to* someone and *loving* someone? What's the difference between the two?

• Paul says in chapter 5, verses 28 and 29 that when a husband loves his wife, it's like loving and taking care of his own body. If food and exercise keep the body healthy, what ways of loving and caring keep a marriage relationship healthy?

Come back together as a larger group and share any highlights or questions from your subgroup discussion.

 As a larger group, read Ephesians 6:1-4 again.

Host: Bring out all the supply list items at this time.

Think about the following: If you could construct a trophy for a parent, or for someone who was like a parent to you, what would the trophy be like? What qualities or acts would it honor? (If you had a tough relationship with your parents, don't get wrapped up in that right now—either find something about them you can honor, or choose someone who was a surrogate parent to you to honor instead.)

Using the items supplied—or items you have with you—create a simple trophy that conveys what you want to honor about this person. For instance, you might place a rock on an upside-down cup base to honor a parent who was a "steadying rock" in your life. You can use the modeling clay to sculpt something or to attach items together.

Take five minutes to create your trophies. When you've finished, show them to the group; then answer the following questions:

• What's one thing your trophy says about the person you're honoring?

• What things came to your mind while you were making your trophy?

• Look again at Ephesians 6:2-3. What's significant to you about the fact that the command to honor father and mother includes a promise? What other benefits are there to honoring others?

MAKING IT PERSONAL (15 minutes)

Read Ephesians 6:5-9 again. Look also at the quotes on this page, and answer the following questions:

- On a scale of 1 to 10 (10 being the highest), how much of a slave of Christ are you—really?

- How does "do[ing] the will of God with all your heart" solve many of the problems in *all* the types of relationships mentioned in this session's passage? What would it look like in your own life?

- Whom is it hardest for you to submit to? What makes it so hard? What could you do or say to love, honor, and care for that person in the days and weeks to come?

> "So Jesus called them together and said, 'You know that the rulers in this world lord it over their people, and officials flaunt their authority over those under them. But among you it will be different. Whoever wants to be a leader among you must be your servant, and whoever wants to be first among you must be the slave of everyone else. For even the Son of Man came not to be served but to serve others and to give his life as a ransom for many.'"
> —Mark 10:42-45

> "This letter is from Paul and Timothy, slaves of Christ Jesus."
> —Philippians 1:1

> "This letter is from James, a slave of God and of the Lord Jesus Christ."
> —James 1:1

TOUCHING YOUR WORLD (25 minutes)

Review the following weekly challenge options, and select the challenge you'd like to do. Turn to a partner, and share your choice. Then make plans to connect with your partner sometime between now and the next session to check in and encourage one another.

☐ **PRAY A PRAYER OF SUBMISSION EACH MORNING.**
Start each day with a prayer like "Lord, I give myself totally to you this day. Show me where my will needs to be molded by yours." Be sensitive to opportunities where God wants to answer your prayer, especially where submitting to God's will might also require submitting to another person. Take time at the end of each day to evaluate how this approach has changed your behavior.

☐ **WRITE A LETTER TO A PARENT.** Honor your mom or dad (or both) for the positive things he or she did for you. You can do this even if your parent is no longer living. In such a case, rather than mailing the letter, put it in a special place and preserve it.

☐ **GIVE A FAMILY MEMBER THE GIFT OF A CHOICE.** In a situation where *you* might normally choose the movie or restaurant the family goes to, or music the family listens to on a road trip, let another family member choose. (If you let one of your children choose, reserve the right to veto anything you deem inappropriate.) Observe how this "gift" affects your family member.

☐ **SUPPORT ACTION AGAINST DOMESTIC ABUSE.** One of the great tragedies of life today is that not everyone follows Paul's advice in caring for family. Contact a domestic abuse organization and see what you can do to support its efforts to fight such abuse.

Southern Valley Alliance — Check any needs

Come back together as a group. Share prayer requests. Also, if you're comfortable doing so, share the weekly challenges you've committed to this week and make these "points of prayer." Then pray together for everyone's needs.

Until next time...

Date _____

Time _____

Place _____

Taking It Home:

1. Set a goal for how many times you'll either read through or watch on your DVD the Session 8 Bible passage (Ephesians 6:10-24). Make a point to read the "A Sense of History" feature in Session 8 (page 84) before the next session. You may also want to review this week's passage—or even watch the entire book of Ephesians straight through. (It takes about 22 minutes.) Let your weekly challenge partner know what goals you've set, so he or she can encourage you and help hold you accountable.

2. Touch base sometime before the next session with your weekly challenge partner to compare notes on how you're both doing with the goals you've set.

3. If you have volunteered for a role or signed up to help with food or supplies for the next session, be sure to prepare for this. The Session 8 Supplies list can be found on page 80, and the Food Coordinator instructions are on page 107.

4. **I commit to touching my world this week by loving, caring for, and honoring those around me in the following ways:**

_____

_____

_____

_____

SESSION 8:

PREPARING FOR BATTLE

EPHESIANS 6:10-24

In this session you'll discover how to recognize the spiritual battles that all Christians face, and how you can prepare for those battles.

PRE-SESSION CHECKLIST:

☐ **Leader:** Check out the Session 8 Leader Notes in the back of the book (page 102).

☐ **Food Coordinator:** If you are responsible for the Session 8 snack, see page 107.

☐ **Supplies:**

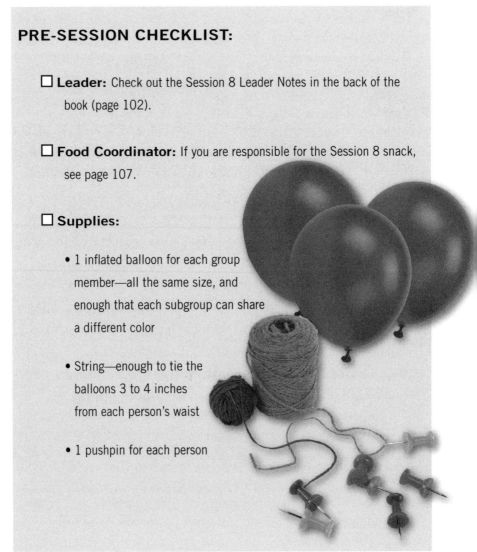

- 1 inflated balloon for each group member—all the same size, and enough that each subgroup can share a different color

- String—enough to tie the balloons 3 to 4 inches from each person's waist

- 1 pushpin for each person

TASTE AND SEE (20 minutes)

For today's snack, you have a choice—angel food cake or devil's food cake. No allegiance is implied here!

> **Did you know?**
>
> Devil's food cake is usually thought of in terms of dark chocolate, but originally it was red. The cake dates back at least to 1902, when it appeared in Mrs. Rorer's New Cook Book. The cake was popular in the Southern United States, where it was originally made from beets and cocoa.

While you're enjoying your snack, discuss the following questions:

• Which cake did you choose? Why?

• Why do you think these two cakes became associated with angels and devils? Do you think they've earned their names?

Watch the final chapter on the DVD (Ephesians 6:10-24).

Ephesians 6:10-24

[10]A final word: Be strong in the Lord and in his mighty power. [11]Put on all of God's armor so that you will be able to stand firm against all strategies of the devil. [12]For we are not fighting against flesh-and-blood enemies, but against evil rulers and authorities of the unseen world, against mighty powers in this dark world, and against evil spirits in the heavenly places.

[13]Therefore, put on every piece of God's armor so you will be able to resist the enemy in the time of evil. Then after the battle you will still be standing firm. [14]Stand your ground, putting on the belt of truth and the body armor of God's righteousness. [15]For shoes, put on the peace that comes from the Good News so that you will be fully prepared. [16]In addition to all of these, hold up the shield of faith to stop the fiery arrows of the devil. [17]Put on salvation as your helmet, and take the sword of the Spirit, which is the word of God.

[18]Pray in the Spirit at all times and on every occasion. Stay alert and be persistent in your prayers for all believers everywhere.

[19]And pray for me, too. Ask God to give me the right words so I can boldly explain God's mysterious plan that the Good News is for Jews and Gentiles alike. [20]I am in chains now, still preaching this message as God's ambassador. So pray that I will keep on speaking boldly for him, as I should.

21To bring you up to date, Tychicus will give you a full report about what I am doing and how I am getting along. He is a beloved brother and faithful helper in the Lord's work. 22I have sent him to you for this very purpose—to let you know how we are doing and to encourage you.

23Peace be with you, dear brothers and sisters, and may God the Father and the Lord Jesus Christ give you love with faithfulness. 24May God's grace be eternally upon all who love our Lord Jesus Christ.

A SENSE OF HISTORY
Armed for Battle

In Paul's time, body armor for Roman soldiers was extensive. The first line of defense was an oval shield made from layers of wood glued together, with one layer of wood running in the opposite grain from the next. The outside of the shield was covered with leather, and its edges were bound with bronze or iron.

If a weapon got past that protection and was aimed at the head, it encountered a protective helmet, which was usually made of bronze with an iron skull plate inside it. This helmet had projections protecting the neck and forehead, with cheek guards protecting the jaw. If the enemy's weapon got past the shield and was aimed at the body, the soldier was protected by body armor. A sleeveless jacket of hardened leather covered with strips of metal protected the upper body, and many soldiers supplemented this with leg guards.

Of the offensive weapons available, the principle one was a double-edged, approximately 2-foot-long sword. It was carried in a scabbard suspended on the right-hand side from a girdle around the waist, and supported by a shoulder strap.

No soldier fights effectively by staying on the defensive, and thus the weapons of a Christian in spiritual war include both defensive and offensive weapons. Armed with the Word of God, Christians can take the offensive to win victories for Jesus—not through violence and bloodshed, but through love and truth.

DIGGING INTO SCRIPTURE (30 minutes)

As a group, discuss:

• What thoughts or emotions came to your mind while watching this session's Bible passage?

• What have your overall impressions been as you've interacted with the book of Ephesians? How has God spoken to you through this study?

Now break into subgroups.

Subgroup Leaders: Take up to 15 minutes for your discussion time. Read Ephesians 6:10-24, and answer the following questions:

• What's your reaction to Paul's statement in verse 12 that we are fighting "against mighty powers in this dark world, and against evil spirits in the heavenly places"? Does it make you frightened and insecure? challenged and really pumped? skeptical? something else?

• Paul refers to seven spiritual weapons in verses 14-18—truth, righteousness, peace, faith, salvation, the Word of God, and prayer. Which of these weapons do you find yourself using the most in your own battles?

• Which spiritual weapons could you use an "upgrade" in? Who or what could help you get those upgrades?

Come back together as a larger group and share any highlights or questions from your subgroup discussions.

Team up with your subgroups.

Host: Bring out the balloons, string, and pushpins.

Take note: Normally we are discouraged from "bursting each other's balloon." In fact the Greek word for wind, air, and spirit is the same: pneuma. Therefore, to "burst someone's balloon" is to deflate their spirit. But try not to deflate anyone's spirit while you pop the balloons!

Each subgroup should select a balloon color. Each person should have one pushpin and should also tie one balloon 3 or 4 inches from his or her waist.

The object is to pop the other teams' balloons without getting the balloons on your team popped. If your balloon is popped, sit down—you're out of the battle.

Before you start, take one minute to formulate a strategy with your team. Then get started! Play nicely—no pushing, shoving, or grabbing is allowed.

When the balloon battle is over, discuss the following questions:

• What strategy worked best in this battle?

• How do you see the devil or forces of evil trying to "burst *your* balloon"?

• What strategies do you see being used against you—in other words, what do you see as your spiritual "hot buttons"?

Did you know?

The sound of a balloon popping is actually a sonic boom! When a tiny hole is made in a balloon, the retracting of the stretched balloon latex causes the hole to grow faster than the speed of sound in air, causing a small sonic boom.

• Knowing where you're most susceptible to attack, how can you adjust your battle plan so you can more effectively fight your spiritual battles?

MAKING IT PERSONAL (15 minutes)

Read Ephesians 6:11-18 one more time, and then answer the following questions:

- When was a time you weren't fully prepared for spiritual battle? What was the result? What did you learn from that experience?

- What are some of the spiritual battles you currently see around you—or in your own life?

- What are practical ways you can "put on every piece of God's armor" and respond to those battles?

TOUCHING YOUR WORLD (25 minutes)

Review the following weekly challenge options, and then select the challenge you'd like to do. Turn to a partner, and share your choice. Then make plans to connect with your partner in the next week to check in and encourage one another.

☐ **USE YOUR "SWORD" EVERY DAY.** If you're not already reading your Bible regularly, commit to a goal of reading it for five minutes a day. If you're already reading your Bible regularly, increase your goal. Think of it as honing the sword of the Word of God.

☐ **IDENTIFY WEAK AREAS WHICH NEED TO BE "SHIELDED."** Where have you been most susceptible to attack in the past? Sexual temptation? Addiction? The lure of materialism and greed? Commit to staying away from places where temptation is likely, and to praying for that area of your life daily. Ask for God's special strength, and find a person who will hold you accountable in that area. You might be sitting with him or her right now.

☐ **BECOME AN ALLY TO SOMEONE UNDER SPIRITUAL ATTACK.** Who do you know who seems to be under a great deal of spiritual pressure? Maybe he or she is facing harassment by persons with a destructive agenda; maybe he or she is encountering more than a usual amount of temptation; or maybe he or she is just going through a tough time. Focus your prayers on this individual in the week to come. Be sensitive to other ways you can support the person, such as sending a note of encouragement or personally intervening on his or her behalf.

Come back together as a group, and re-read Ephesians 6:18. Then ask group members to take a minute of silence to visualize people they know who need to be included in the phrase "for all believers everywhere."

Afterward, share prayer requests, and pray for everyone's needs. Take time also to thank God for all he has done in your group members' lives during this study.

Leader: If you haven't already, take some time to discuss what's next for the group. Will you stay together and work on another BibleSense book? Will you celebrate your time together with a party and just be done? Or will you have a party, and *then* start another BibleSense book the following week?

Touch-base time:

Set a date, time, and place to get together with your weekly challenge partner during the next week.

Date _____

Time _____

Place _____

Taking It Home:

1. Touch base during the week with your weekly challenge partner to compare notes on how you're both doing with the goals you've set.

2. You may want to review this week's passage—or even watch the entire book of Ephesians straight through on your DVD, now that you've finished your study. (It takes about 22 minutes to watch the entire book.)

3. **I commit to touching my world this week by preparing for spiritual battle in the following ways:**

_____

_____

_____

_____

_____

NOTES & ROLES

CONTENTS

LEADER NOTES

GROUP ROLES

GENERAL LEADER TIPS

1. Although these sessions are designed to require minimum advance preparation, try to read over each session ahead of time and watch the relevant DVD chapter. Highlight any questions you feel are especially important for your group to spend time on during the session.

2. Prior to the first session, watch the "Leading a BibleSense Session" overview on the DVD. You'll notice that this isn't your average Bible study. Food? Activities? Don't forget that Jesus used food and everyday items and experiences in *his* small group all the time. Jesus' disciples certainly weren't comfortable when he washed their feet (John 13:4-17) and were even a bit confused at first. Jesus reassured them, "You don't understand now what I am doing, but someday you will" (verse 7), and it turned out to be a powerful lesson that stayed with them the rest of their lives. It's our prayer that your group will have similar experiences.

3. Take the time to read the group roles on pages 103-111, and make sure all critical tasks and roles are covered for each session. The three roles you *absolutely need filled* for each session are Leader, Host, and Food Coordinator. These roles can be rotated around the group, if you like.

4. Discuss as a group how to handle child care—not only because it can be a sensitive subject, but to give your group an opportunity to begin working together *as* a group. See the Child Care Coordinator tips on page 111 for ideas on how to handle this important issue.

5. Don't be afraid to ask for volunteers. Who knows—they may want to commit to a role once they've tried it (and if it's available on a regular basis). However, give people the option of "no thanks" as well.

6. Every session will begin with a snack, so work closely with your Food Coordinator—he or she has a vital role in each session. If you need to, go ahead

and ask for donations from your group for the snacks that are provided each week.

7. Always start on time. If you do this from Session 1, you'll avoid the group arriving and starting later and later as the study goes on.

8. Be ready and willing to pray at times other than the closing time. Start each session with prayer—let everyone know they're getting "down to business." Be open to other times where prayer is appropriate, such as when someone answers a question and ends up expressing pain or grief over a situation he or she is currently struggling with. Don't save it for the end—stop and pray right there and then. Your Prayer Coordinator can take the lead in these situations, if you like, but give him or her "permission" to do so.

9. Try not to have the first or last word on every question (or even most of them). Give everyone the opportunity to participate. At the same time, don't put anyone on the spot—remind group members that they can "pass" on any questions they're not comfortable answering.

10. Keep things on track. There are suggested time limits for each section. Encourage good discussion, but don't be afraid to "rope 'em back in." If you do decide to spend extra time on a question or activity, consider skipping or spending less time on a later question or activity so you can stay on schedule.

11. Don't let your group off the hook with the assignments in the "Touching Your World" section—this is when group members get to apply, in a personal way, what they've learned. Encourage people to follow through on their assignments. You may even want to make it a point to ask how they did with their weekly challenges during snack time at the beginning of your next session.

12. Also note that the last weekly challenge in "Touching Your World" is often an outreach assignment that can be done either individually or as a group. Make sure that group members who take on these challenges are encouraged—and, if it's a group activity, organized. If your group has an Outreach Coordinator, let him or her take the lead here, and touch base regularly.

13. Lastly, research has shown that the single most important thing a leader can do for his or her group is to spend time in prayer for group members. Why not take a minute and pray for your group right now?

Session 1 Leader Notes

1. Read the General Leader Tips starting on page 93, if you haven't already. Take a peek at the tips for other group roles as well (pages 103-111).

2. Make sure everyone has a BibleSense book and DVD. Have the group pass around their books to record contact information (page 7), either before or during "Taste and See" or at the end of the session.

3. If this is the first time you're meeting as a group, you may want to take a few minutes before your session to lay down some ground rules. Here are three simple ones:

- Don't say anything that will embarrass anyone or violate someone's trust.
- Likewise, anything shared in the group *stays* in the group, unless the person sharing it says otherwise.
- No one has to answer a question he or she is uncomfortable answering.

4. Take time to review the group roles on pages 103-111 before you get together, and be ready to discuss them at the end of your session. Assign as many roles as you can, but don't pressure anyone to take on something he or she doesn't want or isn't yet sure about.

5. For this session, *you're* responsible for the items in the Supplies list on page 8. For future sessions, you'll want to assign the Supplies list. The Host is the most obvious choice to handle this responsibility, or it can be rotated around the group.

6. Unless you're ahead of the game and already have a Food Coordinator, *you're* responsible for the snack for this first session. You'll want to make sure you have a Food Coordinator for future sessions, but for this session be sure to review the Food Coordinator assignment on page 106.

7. Before you dismiss this first session, make a special point to remind group members of the importance of following through on the weekly challenge each of them have committed to in the "Touching Your World" section.

8. Read over the "Touching Your World" section. If members of your group choose to do the activity in "Share the blessings, part 3," use part of your prayer time to pray for where and how God would want your group to serve. Select a time and a place to gather the items, and be sure they're distributed in a timely manner. If your group has an Outreach Coordinator, you may want to ask him or her to take the responsibility here. If so, set this up in advance.

Session 2 Leader Notes

1. If new people join the group this session, use part of the "Taste and See" time to ask them to introduce themselves to the group, and have the group pass around their books to record contact information (page 7). Give a brief summary of the points covered in Session 1.

2. If you told group members during the first session that you'd be following up to see how they did with their "Touching Your World" commitments, be sure to do so. This is an opportunity to establish an environment of accountability. However, be prepared to share how *you* did with your own commitment from the first session.

3. Look over the sensory experience in "Digging Into Scripture." Ask group members to bring boxes with them, if needed. Also think about ways you can celebrate the tearing down of your group's wall when you're finished. Raise a toast, give a mock eulogy, do the wave—whatever fits your group's personality best. Take a few moments to celebrate before moving on!

4. Look at the last "Making It Personal" question, and the reflection time immediately afterward. Ask everyone to reflect and pray silently. After a minute or two, say "amen," and move on to "Touching Your World."

5. Read over the "Connect with an 'outsider' " option in "Touching Your World." If someone selects this option, make a point of encouraging him or her before your group gathers again. If you like, set a time during the week when everyone who chose this option can sit down together, compare notes on results so far, and talk about how to follow up. Again, if your group has an Outreach Coordinator, ask that person in advance to handle this responsibility.

6. For the closing prayer time, ask for volunteers to pray for requests that were shared. You may want to ask the Prayer Coordinator in advance, if you have one, to lead the prayer time. If you don't have a Prayer Coordinator, look over the Prayer Coordinator tips on page 104, and keep them in mind if you're leading the prayer time. If you ask someone else to lead it, try to ask them in advance—and direct them to these tips. Also, if your group has decided to make a prayer list, make sure you use it during your prayer time.

Session 3 Leader Notes

1. Take special note of your Food Coordinator's assignment for this session, on page 106. Work together with your Food Coordinator and Host to make sure the surprise involved with this snack goes according to plan.

2. Note this week's Supplies list. Make sure the cup is set up before the group arrives. The pieces of gum should be placed inside the cup, with every stick of gum the same—except one. Also, make sure the total number of pieces of gum in each cup matches the number of people in your group. Don't let anyone peek as they're selecting.

Also, decide in advance where to put your "outsider." Ideally, it will be in another room altogether, but where he or she is near enough to hear the discussion the rest of the group is having. You may want to pick a "hot topic" in advance for your group's "insider" discussion.

Be sure to bring the whole group in welcoming him or her back when you're ready—you could even encourage some hugs and pats on the back.

3. Did any group members select the "Connect with an 'outsider' " option last week? If so, did you or someone else touch base with them this week? If no one has touched base yet, take time to follow up now.

4. Are you praying for your group members regularly? It's the most important thing a leader can do for his or her group. Take some time now to pray for your group, if you haven't already.

Session 4 Leader Notes

1. Congratulations! You're halfway through this study. It's time for a checkup: How's the group going? What's worked well so far? What might you consider changing as you approach the remaining sessions?

2. On that topic, you may find it helpful to make some notes right after your session to help you evaluate how things are going. Ask yourself, "Did everyone participate?" and "Is there anyone I need to make a special effort to follow up with before the next session?"

3. Take special note of the sensory experience in the "Digging Into Scripture" section. Ideally, you'll use the belts that group members are wearing, but have a few extras available just in case. Encourage everyone to participate—it's a true "group-binding" experience!

Session 5 Leader Notes

1. Remember the importance of starting and ending on time, and remind your group of it, too, if you need to.

2. Note the Supplies list for this session. Make sure both jackets are of a good size. As far as the old, beat-up jacket goes: the older, the dirtier, the smellier—the better! Just make sure people's clothes won't get dirty while they're trying it on. (Mention these details to your Host if he or she is responsible for the supplies.)

3. Take special note of the sensory experience and follow-up questions in "Digging Into Scripture" on pages 54-56. If there are non-Christians in your group, the idea of throwing off an "old life" and putting on a new life in Jesus may be totally foreign to them. Be prepared to explain this concept if you need to, but don't preach it. Doing this activity may even offer an opportunity to get together with this person or persons during the next week, to answer questions they might have and open them up further to receiving that new life in Jesus.

Session 6 Leader Notes

1. This would be a good time to remind group members of the importance of following through on the weekly challenge that each of them has committed to in "Touching Your World."

2. Note the sensory experience in "Digging Into Scripture" and "Making It Personal." Keep these rounds of Simon Says moving quickly, so as to keep group members engaged. You could even do "speed rounds" during the "Digging Into Scripture" time, so more people have a chance to lead. Or let one person lead the "Digging Into Scripture" round, but do it in slow motion. However you approach it, keep your "Digging Into Scripture" round to three or four minutes, tops.

3. How are you doing with your prayer time for the group? Take some time to pray for your group now, if you haven't done so already.

Session 7 Leader Notes

1. Since your next session will be your group's last one in this book, you may want to start discussing with the group what to do after you've completed this study.

2. On that note, you may want to do another group checkup before you begin your next study (if that's the plan). Ask yourself, "Is everyone participating?" and "Is there anyone I need to make a special effort to follow up with?"

3. Review the Supplies list; then read over the sensory experience in the "Digging Into Scripture" section to understand how the supplies will be used. Probably nothing will be destroyed in the making of these "trophies," but if you want to use more expendable materials, that's OK. (After all, CDs that have been sitting in modeling clay tend not to play very well afterward!) You can add other items not listed here that you think would work well. You could even call group members in advance and ask them to bring small items that have personal meaning for them (but be sure to explain what they'll be used for).

4. At the end of your sensory experience, we recommend a *brief* show-and-tell time. Let everyone share, but keep things moving.

5. Take time to pray for victims of domestic abuse—as well as for marriages in your church—during your prayer time. Your Prayer Coordinator can lead this time of prayer. It's not necessary to name names, but if someone in your group specifically needs and requests prayer in one of these areas, be sure to pray for him or her. Show sensitivity, but also realize that there is opportunity for some to be released from the pain and shame of abuse, whether it's someone in your group or someone in that situation your group is praying for. **Extra Impact:** Locate information on domestic abuse organizations in your area, and make it available to your group.

Session 8 Leader Notes

1. Since this is your group's last session in this book, make sure you have a plan for next week...and beyond.

2. As part of this last session, you may want to consider having people share, either during the "Taste and See" section or at the end of your session, what this study or group has meant to them. (This can be incorporated into the beginning of your prayer time, if you prefer.)

3. This session deals with the subject of spiritual battles. However, you may have people in your group who aren't yet Christians, for whom "spiritual warfare" may be a foreign concept. It may be a good time to encourage those individuals to take the first step in the battle described here—to make a choice to follow Jesus. Pray for wisdom on how to approach this part.

4. The "Making It Personal" section concludes with a question concerning how each of us can better respond to the spiritual battles in our own lives. Take some extra time with this question. Encourage everyone in the group to brainstorm ideas for each battle that's identified.

5. Here's another suggestion to make the closing prayer time for this last session special. Have the group form a prayer circle. Then have each person or couple, if they're comfortable doing so, take a turn standing or kneeling in the middle of the circle while the group prays specifically for them. Your Prayer Coordinator is a good candidate to lead this time.

GROUP ROLES

ROLE DESCRIPTIONS

Review the group roles that follow.

We have provided multiple roles to encourage maximum participation. At minimum, there are three roles that we recommend be filled for every session: Leader, Food Coordinator, and Host. These particular roles can also be rotated around the group, if you like. Other roles (Outreach and Inreach Coordinators especially) are best handled by only one person per role, as they involve tasks that may take more than one week to accomplish. It's *your* group—you decide what works best. What's most important is that you work together in deciding.

Not everyone will want to take on a role, so no pressure. But as you come to own a role in your group, you'll feel more connected. You'll even become more comfortable with that role that you're not so sure you want to volunteer for right now.

Read through the following roles together, and write in each volunteer's name after his or her role in your book, so everyone remembers who's who (and what roles may still be available).

LEADER _____.

Your session Leader will facilitate each session, keeping discussions and activities on track. If a role hasn't yet been filled or the person who normally has a certain role misses a session, the session Leader will also make sure that all tasks and supplies are covered.

FOOD COORDINATOR _____.

The Food Coordinator will oversee the snacks for each group meeting. This role not only builds the fellowship of the group, but it is an especially important role for this particular study, since specific snacks are assigned for each session and are used to lead group members into the meaning of each session.

HOST _____.

Your Host will open up his or her home—and help group members and visitors feel *at* home. It sounds simple enough, but the gift of hospitality is critical to your group. If group members don't feel welcome, chances are they won't stay group members for long. Your Host should also be responsible for supplying—or locating someone who *can* supply—the items in the Supplies list at the beginning of each session. (They're usually common household items, so don't panic.)

OUTREACH COORDINATOR _____.

Different sessions often highlight different ways to reach out—sharing the Word, extending personal invitations to others to come to your group, or participating in service projects where your group meets the needs of those in your neighborhood or community. Your Outreach Coordinator will champion and coordinate those efforts to reach outside of your group.

GROUP CARE ("INREACH") COORDINATOR _____

_____. Everyone needs a pat on the back once in a while. Therefore, every group also needs a good Inreach Coordinator— someone who oversees caring for the personal needs of group members. That might involve coordinating meals for group members who are sick, making contact with those who have missed a session, arranging for birthday/anniversary celebrations for group members, or sending "just thinking of you" notes.

PRAYER COORDINATOR _____.

Your Prayer Coordinator will record and circulate prayer requests to the rest of the group during the week, as well as channel any urgent prayer requests to the group (that may come up during the week). He or she may also be asked to lead the group in prayer at the close of a session.

SUBGROUP LEADER(S) _____

_____.

To maximize participation, and also to have enough time to work through the session, at various points we recommend breaking into smaller subgroups of three or four persons. Therefore, you'll need Subgroup Leaders. This is also a great opportunity to develop leaders within the group (who may potentially like to lead new groups in the future).

CHILD CARE COORDINATOR _____.

Your Child Care Coordinator will make arrangements to ensure that children are cared for while their parents meet, either at the Host's home or at some other agreed-upon location(s). Depending on the makeup of your group, this could be a make-or-break role in getting new people to come to the sessions.

To emphasize again, if you don't have volunteers for every role (aside from Leader, Food Coordinator, and Host), that's OK. You may need to think about it first or become more comfortable before making a commitment. What's important is that once you commit to a role, you keep that commitment. If you know you'll miss a session, give the session Leader as much advance notice as possible so your role can be covered.

Whether you volunteer for a role now, or want to think things over, take time before the next session to look over the "Group Role Tips" section that begins on the following page. You'll find plenty of useful ideas that will help your group and your role in it (or the role you're considering) be the best they can be.

GROUP ROLE TIPS

FOOD COORDINATOR

1. Sometimes your snack will be a surprise to the rest of the group. Be sure to work closely with your Host and Leader so the timing of your snacks helps this session be the best it can be.

2. You may also need to arrive a few minutes early to set up the surprise. Arrange a time with the Host for your arrival before the meeting.

FOOD COORDINATOR ASSIGNMENTS AND IDEAS

Session 1

Provide food and drink that everyone will think of as a "blessing." It could be something fancy, such as smoked salmon on crackers or fine chocolates, or it could be just a huge assortment of homemade goodies. The important thing is to "wow" your group for this first session.

Session 2

For today's snack, you'll want to provide two distinctly different treats, each on a separate platter:

- A healthy treat that's maybe not so attractive (such as celery sticks or a vegetable platter)
- Another snack that's not healthy, but is very attractive (such as chocolate)

Session 3

This week you'll need to make giant cookies. Prepare your favorite cookie recipe, roll the dough into one giant heart or circle, and bake it. Be sure you make at least two giant cookies.

Put only *one* cookie out at the beginning of the study. Serve your group, make a show of cutting large slices for the people who are first in line...*and make sure you run out of the snack before everyone has been served.*

Wait for your have-nots to react—but don't wait *too* long! Then pull out the second cookie (and third, if necessary). Continue serving until everyone has a slice of cookie.

Session 4

You'll need to serve the following:

- One platter of sweet-tasting fruit, such as apples, oranges, or grapes (you could even put some sugar on the side)
- One platter of sour fruits and vegetables, such as lemons, limes, pickles, or olives

Make each platter equally attractive and of equal size, so the difference between them isn't readily obvious—until group members start thinking about the choices they've made.

Session 5

For this session, you'll need the following:

- A few packages of ready-made cookie dough
- Two packages of ready-to-bake bread

Before the group meets, bake *one* of the loaves of bread and *half* of the cookie dough. Prepare some of the remaining cookie dough to be only half-baked, and leave some of it totally *un*baked. Do the same for your bread dough—leave some dough completely *un*baked, and bake the rest of it only partially.

Session 6

You will need to serve several smaller bags (or one *large* bag) of trail mix for this session. Be sure each member in the group has at least enough for a handful.

Session 7

You'll need to provide four kinds of ice cream for this session. Make sure they're four very distinct choices ("chocolate" *and* "double-chocolate fudge" doesn't count!). Depending on your group's dietary needs, it may be a good idea to make one choice "light" or "low cal" and provide sherbet as another choice.

Session 8

For this session, prepare both an angel food cake and a devil's food cake. (It's OK to bless both cakes before you start eating them!)

Thanks again for all your work in making this a successful study!

HOST

1. Before your group gets together, make sure the environment is just right. Is the temperature in your home or meeting place comfortable? Is there enough lighting? Are there enough chairs for everyone? Can they be arranged in a way that everyone's included? Is your bathroom clean and "stocked"? Your home doesn't need to win any awards—just don't let anything be a distraction from your time together.

2. Once the session's started, do what you can to keep it from being interrupted. When possible, don't answer the phone. Ask people to turn off their cell phones or pagers, if necessary. If your phone number's an emergency contact for someone in the group, designate a specific person to answer the phone, so the session can continue to run smoothly.

3. If you're responsible for the supplies, be sure to read through the Supplies list before each session. If there's any difficulty in supplying any of the materials, let your Leader know, or contact someone else in the group who you know has them. The items required for each session are usually common household items, so most weeks this will be pretty easy. Make sure everything's set up before the group arrives.

4. Be sure to also check each week what the Food Coordinator's got planned. Sometimes the snack is a surprise, so he or she may need your help in *keeping* it a surprise from the rest of the group. Your Food Coordinator may also need to arrive a few minutes early to set up, so be sure to work out a time for his or her arrival before the meeting.

5. And, of course, make your guests feel welcome. That's your number-one priority as Host. Greet group members at the door, and make them feel at home from the moment they enter. Spend a few minutes talking with them after your session—let them know you see them as people and not just as "group members." Thank them for coming as they leave.

OUTREACH COORDINATOR _____

1. Don't forget: New people are the lifeblood of a group. They will keep things from getting stale, and they'll keep your group outwardly focused—as it should be. Encourage the group to invite others.

2. Don't overlook the power of a personal invitation—even to those who don't know Jesus. Invite people from work or your neighborhood to your group, and encourage other group members to do the same.

3. Take special note of the "Touching Your World" section at the end of each session. The last weekly challenge is often an outreach assignment that can be done either individually or as a group. Be sure to encourage and follow up with group members who take on these challenges.

4. If group members choose an outreach option for their weekly challenge, use part of your closing time together to ask God for help in selecting the right service opportunity and for a blessing upon the group's efforts. Then spend some time afterward discussing what you'll do next.

5. Consider having an event before you begin your BibleSense study (or after you finish it). Give a "no obligation" invitation to Christians and non-Christians alike, just to have the opportunity to meet the others in the group. Do mention, however, what the group will be studying next, so they have an opportunity to consider joining you for your next study. Speak with the Leader before making any plans, however.

6. As part of your personal prayer time, pray that God would bring new people to the group. Make this also a regular part of your group's prayer time.

GROUP CARE ("INREACH") COORDINATOR *Candy*

1. Make a point of finding out more about your group members each week. You should be doing this as a group member, but in your role as Inreach Coordinator, you'll have additional opportunities to use what you learn to better care for those in your group.

2. If a group member has special needs, be sure to contact him or her during the week. If it's something the group can help with, get permission first, and then bring the rest of the group into this ministry opportunity.

3. Find out the special dates, such as birthdays or anniversaries, in your group members' lives. Make or bring cards for other group members to sign in advance.

4. If someone in your group is sick, has a baby, or faces some other kind of emergency, you may want to coordinate meals for that person with the rest of the group.

PRAYER COORDINATOR

1. Pray for your group throughout the week, and encourage group members to pray for one another. Keep a prayer list, and try to send out prayer reminders after each session.

2. Be sure to keep group members up-to-date on any current or earlier prayer requests. Pass on "praise reports" when you have them. Remind them that God not only hears, but *answers,* prayer.

3. Remember that the role is called Prayer *Coordinator,* not "Official Pray-er for the Group" (whether that's what your group would prefer or not). At the same time, some members of the group may be uncomfortable praying aloud. If there are several people who don't mind praying, one person could open your prayer time and another close it, allowing others to add prayers in between. Give everyone who wants to pray the opportunity to do so.

4. Prayers don't have to be complex, and probably shouldn't be. Jesus himself said, "When you pray, don't babble on and on as people of other religions do. They think their prayers are answered merely by repeating their words again and again." (Matthew 6:7)

5. If some group members are intimidated by prayer, begin prayer time by inviting group members to complete a sentence as they pray. For example, ask everyone to finish the following: "Lord, I want to thank you for…"

6. Don't overlook the power of silent prayer. Don't automatically fill "dead spaces" in your prayer time—God may be trying to do that by speaking into that silence. You might even consider closing a session with a time of silent prayer.

SUBGROUP LEADER(S)

1. These sessions are designed to require a minimum of preparation. Nonetheless, be sure to read over each session and watch the DVD in advance, to get comfortable with those sections where you may be responsible for leading a subgroup discussion. Highlight any questions you think are important for your subgroup to spend time on in the next session.

2. Try not to have the first or last word on every question (or even most of them). Give everyone the opportunity to participate. At the same time, don't put anyone on the spot—let subgroup members know they can "pass" on any question

they're not comfortable answering.

3. Keep your subgroup time on track. There are suggested time limits for each section. Encourage good discussion, but don't be afraid to "rope 'em back in." If you do decide to spend extra time on a question or activity, consider skipping or spending less time on a later question or activity so you can stay on schedule.

CHILD CARE COORDINATOR

There are several ways you can approach the important issue of child care. Discuss as a group which alternative(s) you'll use:

1. The easiest approach may be for group members to each make their own child care arrangements. Some might prefer this; others may not be able to afford it on their own. If a parent or couple needs financial assistance, see if someone else in the group can help out in this area.

2. If your meeting area is conducive to it, have everyone bring their children to the meeting, and have on-site child care available so parents can pay on a child-by-child basis.

3. If most or all of your group members have young children, you could also consider rotating child care responsibilities around the group rather than paying someone else.

4. If there are members in your group with older children who are mature enough to watch the younger children, pay them to handle your child care. Maybe they can even do their own lesson. If so, Group Publishing offers a number of great materials for children of all ages—go to www.group.com to find out more.

5. Check to see if the youth group at your church would be interested in providing child care as a fund-raiser.

> It is wise to pre-screen any potential child care worker—paid or volunteer—who is watching children as part of a church-sanctioned activity (including a home Bible study). Your church may already have a screening process in place that can be utilized for your group. If not, Group's Church Volunteer Central network (www.churchvolunteercentral.com) is a great resource, containing ready-made background-check and parental-consent forms, as well as articles and other online resources.